Visual Reference Basics

Internet

America Online
Netscape Navigator
Microsoft Internet Explorer

D1167079

Diana Rain

Acknowledgements

Managing Editor
Jennifer Frew

Technical Editor
Cathy Vesecky

Layout and Design
Shawn Morningstar

Copyright 1998 by DDC Publishing, Inc.
Published by DDC Publishing, Inc.

First DDC Publishing, Inc. Printing

10 9 8 7 6 5 4 3 2 1

Printed in the United States of America.

Netscape™, Netscape™ Communications logo, Netscape™ Communications Corporation, Netscape™ Communications, Netscape Mail™, and Netscape™ Navigator are all trademarks of Netscape™ Communications Corporation.

Microsoft® and Windows® are registered trademarks of the Microsoft Corporation.

Yahoo!™ and Yahoo™ logo are trademarks of Yahoo!™

LYCOS™, LYCOS™ logo are trademarks of LYCOS™.

AltaVista™ and the AltaVista™ logo are trademarks of AltaVista Technology, Inc.

Digital™ and the Digital™ logo are trademarks of Digital Equipment Corporation.

Excite is a service mark of Excite Inc.

Switchboard™ is a trademark of Banyan Systems Inc.

Table of Contents

INTRODUCTION

AMERICA ONLINE

MICROSOFT INTERNET EXPLORER

NETSCAPE COMMUNICATOR

Introduction

The Internet, known as the information super-highway, is a digital revolution on a global scale. The Internet is a global network of networks, a way of connecting computers around the world. Through it, you are connected to millions of people around the world. Few technologies have developed so quickly, captured our imagination so completely, or impacted our world so much as the Internet. In a few short years it has become the backbone of research, the lifeblood of business and finance, and the promise of education. It is sure to play a central role in the way we communicate and share information in the future.

The Internet means different things to different people. It is:

- a global community of computer users
- an enormous library of information
- a vast communications network
- a learning environment
- a way to share a common body of knowledge
- fun to visit

This section provides general information on what you can find on the Internet. For example, it gives you an introduction to newsgroups, e-mail, and searching for information on the Web.

Introduction to the Internet

Read This Before You Start This Book!

The following is essential information needed to understand how the Internet works. In addition to providing a basic definition and history of the Internet, we are also including a list of concepts and terms. Though we have done our best to keep technical jargon to a minimum, there are certain words that will be referred to often throughout this book, as well as throughout your journeys on the Internet, so it is best to get an understanding of them from the start.

Must Haves

This book assumes that you already have a basic understanding of computers and that you have access to an Internet Service Provider. Please read over the list of "must haves" below to ensure that you are ready to connect to the Internet.

- A computer (with a recommended minimum of 16 MB of RAM) and a modem port.
- A modem (with a recommended minimum speed of 14.4 kbps, and suggested speed of 28.8 kbps) that is connected to an analog phone line (assuming you are not using a direct Internet connection through a school, corporation, etc.).
- Established access to the Internet through an online service, independent Internet service provider, etc.
- Access to the browser applications: Netscape Navigator 3.0 and/or Microsoft Explorer 3.0. (If you do not currently have these applications, contact your Internet Service Provider for instructions on how to download them.)
- A great deal of patience. The Internet is a fun and exciting place. But getting connected can be frustrating at times. Expect to run into occasional glitches, to get disconnected from time to time, and to experience occasional difficulty in locating a certain Web site, sending e-mail, etc. The more up-to-date your equipment is, however, the less difficulty you will probably experience.

Cautions

ACCURACY: Be cautious not to believe everything on the Internet. Almost anyone can publish information on the Internet, and since there is no Internet editor or monitor, some information may be false. All information found on the World Wide Web should be checked for accuracy through additional reputable sources.

SECURITY: When sending information over the Internet, be prepared to let the world have access to it. Computer hackers can find ways to access anything that you send to anyone over the Internet, including e-mail. Be cautious when sending confidential information to anyone.

VIRUSES: These small, usually destructive computer programs hide inside of innocent-looking programs. Once a virus is executed, it attaches itself to other programs. When triggered, often by the occurrence of a date or time on the computer's internal clock/calendar, it executes an annoying or damaging function, such as displaying a message on your screen, corrupting your files, or reformatting your hard disk.

Basics

The Internet – What is it?

The Internet is a world-wide network that connects several thousands of businesses, schools, research foundations, individuals, and other networks. Anyone with access can log on, communicate via e-mail, and search for various types of information.

Internet History

The Internet began in 1969 as ARPAnet, a project developed by the US Department of Defense. Its initial purpose was to enable researchers and military personnel to communicate in the event of an emergency.

How to Access the Internet

Most people access the Internet by using a modem, communication software, and a standard phone line to dial in. Direct access is also available through most colleges and universities and through some large organizations and corporations.

If you plan to use a dial-in connection to the Internet you will need to sign up with a public or private Internet Service Provider, or an online Service such as America Online, CompuServe, or Delphi. For a certain fee, such services generally provide you with a Web browser, an e-mail account, a predetermined number of hours for Internet access time (or unlimited access at a higher fee), and various other features.

Common Uses of the Internet

- Communicate world wide via e-mail.
- Use the World Wide Web to order products, read reviews, obtain stock quote information, make travel arrangements, do research for work or school projects, etc.
- FTP to a computer site to download or upload shareware items (software, fonts, games, etc.).
- Access a search engine to find Internet sites containing news articles that relate to a particular topic, subject, or product you need information about. See **Download: FTP** on the next page.

Internet Terms

The following is a list of basic terms that will help you start to understand the Internet.

World Wide Web (WWW)

The WWW is a user-friendly system for finding information on the Internet through the use of hypertext and hypermedia linking.

Hyperlinks

On the Web, some words or graphics appear in a different color, are underlined, or both. This distinction indicates that the item is a link to another Web page or another Web site. Clicking your mouse on one of these links takes you to a new page with related information.

Home Page

All Web sites begin with a Home Page. A Home Page is like a table of contents. It usually outlines what a particular site has to offer and contains links that can connect you to other Web pages and sites.

Network

Networks are groups of computers or other devices that are connected in such a way that they are able to share files and resources. The Internet is a global network of networks.

Browsers

Web browsers are graphic interface programs that provide simple techniques for viewing and searching the WWW. Browsers work in conjunction with the connection you establish to the Internet via your Internet service provider. The browser programs referred to in this book are Netscape Navigator and Microsoft Internet Explorer.

URL (Uniform Resource Locators)

A URL is a WWW address. It is a locator that enables the WWW system to search for linked sites. See **URL: Internet Site Addresses.**

Download: FTP (File Transfer Protocol)

FTP (File Transfer Protocol) is the Internet standard for copying files between computers. Downloading a file copies it from a server on the Internet to your computer.

When you download a file (such as a software program) from the Internet, the file is copied to your computer. When you upload a file (such as a Web page), the file is copied from your computer to a computer on the Internet. Files are copied using FTP. You do not have to know anything about FTP, because the process is taken care of for you by your Web browser and the software on the network.

Software on the Internet

You will find three kinds of software available for downloading on the Internet: freeware, shareware, and software for purchase.

Many of the software titles you find on the Net are free for anyone to use. Free software, or free-ware, does not need to be purchased, requires no license, and can be freely copied and distributed. You can find everything from animated cursors to full-blown word processors, all free.

Many titles on the Internet are shareware. When you download shareware, you can use the software free for a trial period, usually limited to 30 days. At that time you either buy the software or delete it from your computer.

Some companies offer software for purchase. For example, you can purchase Microsoft products through retailers on the Internet. You pay for the software with your credit card when you download it.

Using FTP

When you download a file, the process differs little from copying a file. When you click on a file to download from the Internet, most programs display a dialog box, usually named "Download" or "Save." In this dialog box, you select the folder on your computer to copy the file to and the filename that you want to use. It is that easy.

Viruses

Be warned. The Internet is a breeding ground for computer viruses. Be vigilant about checking all files for viruses.

Computer viruses, introduced to your computer through files that you have downloaded, can be very destructive to your system. If you do not have a virus-checking program, download one from Shareware.com (see **Download: Shareware.com**).

File Compression

Most files that you download have been compressed to save disk space and download time. PKZip and WinZip are popular file compression programs. These utilities create compressed files with a .zip extension. You must have a copy of the file compression software used to compress the file in order to expand it. You can download PKZip and WinZip from Shareware.com (see **Download: Shareware.com**). Send in your registration fee for the program after a trial period.

Download: Shareware.com

One of the most popular and useful sites to find software for downloading from the Internet is the Shareware.com page. You can find and download all types of programs at this site.

Go to Shareware.com

Using your Web browser, go to the following address: **http://shareware.com**

Type a search phrase, pick a platform from the drop-down list, and click the Search button

Browse the latest software releases

Browse the software that has been downloaded by the most users in the past week

Read reviews and comparisons of the latest releases of Web browsers and download a browser

Search all software titles

Access Help pages

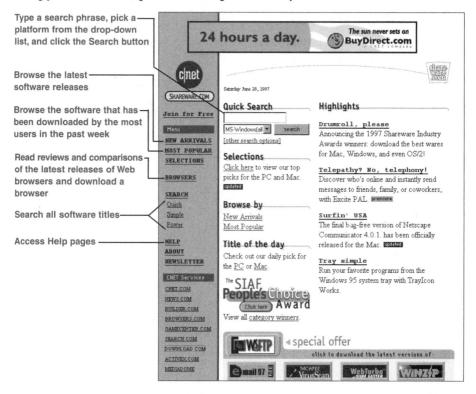

NOTE: To purchase retail software and hardware from companies throughout North America, go to the Shop Computer ESP site at http://www.computeresp.com/. This site scans companies for the best prices, so your comparison shopping is done for you. It includes product reviews.

E-Mail: An Overview

E-mail is one of the most frequently used features of the Internet. Many people sign up for Internet service just so that they can send and receive e-mail messages.

E-mail Addresses

All users who send and receive mail through the Internet must have a unique Internet e-mail address. When you send mail to someone, you send it to their e-mail address so that the message can be routed to the correct person. Your service provider will give you an e-mail address or tell you how to request one.

Although there are exceptions, an Internet e-mail address consists of a user name or ID, @, and a domain name. For example, the Internet address for an America Online user might be: *jdoe2@aol.com*. The user ID (*jdoe2*) identifies the individual and the domain name (*aol.com*) identifies the service provider.

When members of an online service such as America Online send e-mail messages to each other, the @ and the domain information in the address are dropped. For example, if you are sending mail through AOL to user *jdoe2* who is another AOL member, you simply send the mail to the user name *jdoe2*. When sending to a recipient outside of your online service, you must use the full Internet address so that the mail can be routed to the correct domain (such as the AOL domain).

Sending and Receiving Mail

When someone sends you a message, it is routed to your mailbox on the mail server maintained by your service provider. Mail is sent over the Internet using the Simple Mail Transfer Protocol (SMTP). You can read the mail online while it remains on the server or you can retrieve (download) it onto your hard disk. Mail that has been read and/or retrieved from the mail server is automatically deleted from the server by the service provider software.

Address Book

Your e-mail program will have an address book feature that allows you to store e-mail addresses for the people and companies with whom you correspond. Some programs automatically add addresses to your address book whenever you receive mail for the first time from a correspondent. If you maintain an address book, you can quickly select recipient(s) from the address book when you create e-mail messages.

See also

Information on using e-mail in America Online, Netscape Navigator, and Internet Explorer is included in those sections. For smileys and acronyms that you will encounter in e-mail messages, see **Emoticons and Abbreviations**. For tips on e-mail message content, see **Netiquette**.

Emoticons and Abbreviations

Since you can not see the people with whom you are communicating on the Net, here are some symbols you can use to convey emotion in your messages. This section also contains some acronyms that you will encounter in Internet messages (such as e-mail, newsgroup messages, and chat room discussions).

Emoticons

Use these symbols to convey emotions in your message. To see the faces in these symbols, turn the page to the right.

For a complete list of emoticons, go to the Smiley Dictionary Web page at *http://www.pd.nettuno.it/lama/ds/en_smiley.html*.

>:->	Angry		:/)	Not funny
5:-)	Elvis		:-(	Sad
:(	Frown		:-@	Scream
:-)	Happy		:-#	Secret (lips are sealed)
( )	Hug		:P	Sticking tongue out
(((( ))))	Many hugs		:-o	Surprised
:*	Kiss		:-J	Tongue in cheek
:D	Laugh		;-)	Wink
:-?	Licking lips			

A Few Abbreviations

BTW By the way

FYI For your information

IMHO In my humble (or honest) opinion

LOL Laughed out loud (at what you wrote)

RTFM Read the manual. You will get this message if you ask questions in a game, newsgroup, or other area that have already been answered in FAQ lists, help systems, and other easily accessible locations.

TIA Thanks in advance

For a complete list of acronyms, abbreviations, and terms that you will encounter in Internet messages, go to *http://www.erols.com/amato1/AC/* on the Web.

Netiquette

Netiquette is the art of civilized communications between people on the Internet. Whenever you send an e-mail message, a chat room message, or a newsgroup message follow these guidelines.

A Few Tips

- Always include a subject in the message heading. This makes it easy for the recipient to organize messages in folders by topic and to find a message by browsing through message headers.

- Do not use capital letters. To the recipient, it feels like YOU ARE SHOUTING. Instead, enclose text that you want to emphasize with asterisks. For example: *I *meant* Friday of *next* week.*

- Be careful with the tone you use. With the absence of inflection, it is easy to send a message that can be misinterpreted by the recipient. Use emoticons to establish your intent (see **Emoticons and Abbreviations**). A smiley emoticon can make it clear to the recipient that really, you are just joking.

- Spell check your messages before you send them. They represent you.

- Do not send flame messages. These are obnoxious, offensive, or otherwise disturbing messages. If you send this type of message to a newsgroup, the 30,000 people who read your flame will think less of you. If you receive flame mail, probably the best thing you can do is go for the Delete button rather than the Reply button.

- Messages sent over the Internet are not private. You message is in writing and nothing can prevent someone from forwarding it to anyone they please. Assume that anyone with a computer has the potential to read your message.

- Never initiate or forward a chain letter. Some service providers will cancel your membership if you do so, as they are trying to protect their members from unwanted mail.

- If you send a long message it is a good idea to tell the recipient at the beginning of the message so that they can decide if they would rather download it to read later.

The Netiquette Home Page

To connect to sites covering netiquette, visit Albion's Netiquette Home Page at *http://www.albion.com/netiquette/index.html.* The page lists hyperlinks to pages on Netiquette contributed by Internet users. You will find interesting, amusing, and very important material in these sites.

Newsgroups: An Overview

A newsgroup is an ongoing discussion on a particular topic. Newsgroup members post messages, often called articles, to contribute to the discussion. Newsgroups are in an area of the Internet called Usenet.

Getting Started with Newsgroups

If you are new to newsgroups, read the articles in the *news.announce.newusers*, *news.answers*, and *news.newusers.questions* newsgroups. Send general questions about newsgroups to the moderated newsgroup called *news.newusers.questions* but don't send questions before you read the newusers groups. The answer to your question is probably posted in one of these groups. You can search messages in these groups to find answers.

Do not participate in a newsgroup until you have read the FAQ (frequently asked questions) article for the group. Most FAQ articles are available in the group discussion. If you cannot find it there, many groups post their FAQ articles in the *news.announce.newusers* newsgroup.

You can access a Web page with information for new newsgroup users from the DejaNews Web page. See **Newsgroups: DejaNews**.

Netiquette for Newsgroups

Most of your responses to newsgroup messages will be in the form of private e-mail messages sent to the sender of the original message. Before you post a message to the group discussion, make sure your message is relevant and contributes to the discussion. Newsgroups where the interesting information is buried in irrelevant messages are of little interest.

When you post a request for information, request that replies be sent to your e-mail address. After you have received responses, write up a summary of any interesting information that was sent to you and post it to the group.

Your signature should be no more than three lines in length and should not include a graphic. Some newsgroup members routinely download new newsgroup messages and appreciate not having to download lengthy signatures over and over. Also, some newsreaders are slow and larger messages take a longer time to open.

If you get a reply to one of your messages that contains the acronym, RTFM, the sender of the message is telling you that your question is easily answered by reading the FAQ articles or one of the new user groups. The acronym stands for Read the Manual.

Don't send your message to a large number of newsgroups. Each newsgroup is a forum for the free exchange of ideas on a specific topic of interest. Mass mailings of irrelevant material damages the integrity of a newsgroup.

For additional tips on guidelines for composing newsgroup messages, see **Netiquette**.

Newsgroup Categories

When you first see a list of the newsgroups on a server, the newsgroup names do not appear to be related to the content of the group. Once you understand a little about naming conventions used in newsgroups, however, you can more easily find your way around.

The letters in a newsgroup name up to the first period identify the category. This list of categories is not complete. Some servers will have more categories.

alt. and **misc.** Anything not covered in other groups. For example, **misc.misc** is a newsgroup that defies all categories.

comp. Computers.

news. Information about Usenet newsgroups, such as FAQ lists for individual groups, netiquette, updates on groups, and information on how to get started using newsgroups. Example: *news.newusers.questions* is a forum where new users can get their questions answered.

rec. Recreational topics, such as hobbies and entertainment, sports, and movies.

sci. Science topics.

soc. Social issues.

talk. Opinions on any topic.

To find newsgroups by topic, see **Newsgroups: DejaNews**.

Newsgroups: DejaNews

If you are not sure where to start in Usenet or if you want to locate a newsgroup that focuses on a particular topic, use the DejaNews Web page to find newsgroups and browse through messages in newsgroup discussions.

Go to DejaNews

1 Using your Web browser, go to the following address: **http://dejanews.com**

2 To get help on using the page to locate articles and newsgroups, click **New Users!**

3 To find an article or a newsgroup:

a. Type one or more search keywords in the **Quick Search** text box.

b. Click **Find Articles** or **Find Newsgroups**.

c. Click the **Find** button. A list of articles or newsgroups that contains the keyword(s) that you entered is displayed.

*NOTES: To get help on searching, click the **Quick Search** hyperlink.*

*To perform a more complex search and to see details on articles/newsgroups in the search results list, click the **Power Search** hyperlink.*

4 To browse through the list of found articles/newsgroups, click desired hyperlinks.

NOTE: You can also use the Netscape news page to find newsgroups, general information on Usenet, and tips for setting up Netscape Communicator to access newsgroups. The address is: http://home.netscape.com/eng/mozilla/2.0/news/news.html

Search Pages: An Overview

The Web is a vast source of information, but you must be able to search effectively in order to find the information you need. To locate information on the Internet, you should use a search page.

Search Pages

A search page uses a search engine to build a catalog (such as an index or category list) of web resources. A search engine is a software program that goes out on the Web seeking sites and cataloging them based on the words found in the site. You search the catalog for topics of interest to you. Search engines continually visit sites on the Internet to keep information as current as possible.

Each search page uses a different search engine. Therefore, you can perform the same search using different search pages and come up with different results. There is not one single search page that indexes every single site on the Web. Some search engines, such as Metacrawler, create their catalog by searching other search pages in order to return a more comprehensive list.

> NOTE: There are many, many search pages on the Web. For a comparison of search engines, see the Best of the Internet Search Engines site at http://www.clark.net/pub/lschank/web/search.html#net

All search pages include a hyperlink to help pages that tell you how to use the site. Always read the help pages when you use a new search page. You will learn how to perform useful searches using that particular search engine.

The **Search Pages** sections of this book describe a number of popular pages that Internet users go to in order to find information. See also **Download: Shareware.com** to find software and other files that you can download. To locate people and businesses around the world, including e-mail addresses, see **Search Pages: Switchboard**. **Newsgroups: DejaNews** tells you how to find a newsgroup by searching for topics of discussion.

Search Phrases

A search page has a text box for you to type search terms to locate topics.

After you type the search phrase and begin the search (typically by clicking a Search button), a list of sites that might be what you are looking for is displayed. This list is called the search results. The sites that most closely match your search phrase are at the top of the list. Each site listed in the search results is a hyperlink to the specified location. Click a hyperlink to go to the site.

If you don't find what you are looking for:

- Check for misspelled words and typing errors in your search phrase.
- Try another search phrase using synonyms and variations of words. If the search results list is too long, use more precise and specific search terms. When you are not specific enough, the search results can be very lengthy and not relevant to your topic.
- Read the online help for the search page so that you know how to enter an effective search phrase using that particular search engine.
- Try a different search page.

Operators in Search Phrases

Operators are used to narrow your search (which means finding fewer, more relevant sites). The most common search operators are the AND, OR, and NOT Boolean operators.

AND   The documents found in the search must contain all of the words joined by the AND operator. AND is often understood. The search phrase *Microsoft Internet Explorer* is identical to *Microsoft AND Internet AND Explorer*.

        NOTE: Use double quotes to restrict the words in a phrase to the phrase itself. Searching for Microsoft Internet Explorer finds documents with these search terms scattered throughout. Searching for "Microsoft Internet Explorer" will not find documents where only Internet Explorer is mentioned even if the document contains the word "Microsoft" somewhere in it.

OR   The documents found in the search must contain at least one of the words joined by the OR operator. For example, the search phrase *Web OR WWW* finds sites where either term is used to refer to the Web.

NOT   This operator excludes terms in a search phrase. For example, the search phrase *orange NOT county* finds documents on the fruit and does not return documents on Orange County.

Different search pages have additional operators that you can use in a search phrase. Read the online help for the page to find available operators.

More Help

In addition to the online help available for each search page, you will find a wealth of information about searching the Web in various guides on the Internet. Here are some places to go for more help:

Beginners Central *http://www.northernwebs.com/bc*

Zen and the Art of the Internet: A Beginners Guide
http://www.cs.indiana.edu/docproject/zen/zen-1.0_toc.html

Yahoo! Surf School *http://www3.zdnet.com/yil/filters/surfjump.html*

Internet Learner's Page *http://www.clark.net/pub/lschank/web/learn.html*

Internet Searching *http://www.clark.net/pub/lschank/web/search.html*

Searching the Internet *http://www2.shef.ac.uk/info_studies/search/search.html*

To find even more helpful sites, connect to a search page and search for *search web*. This will get you to a list of tutorials, guides, search pages, and other information.

Search Pages: AltaVista

The AltaVista search engine "crawls" through sites on the Internet and builds and constantly updates an index of words found in Web pages. This is a fast and powerful search page.

Go To AltaVista

Using your Web browser, go to the following address: **http://www.altavista.digital.com**

Type a search phrase and click the Submit button

History and description of the AltaVista search engine

Show more or fewer details about sites in the search results list

Search the Web or Usenet

Set up a complex search phrase

Help pages

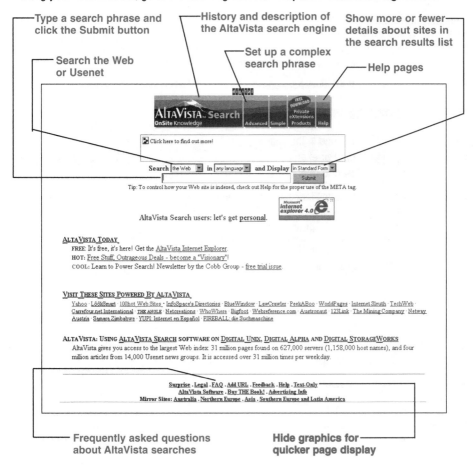

Frequently asked questions about AltaVista searches

Hide graphics for quicker page display

Search Pages: Lycos

Lycos provides a powerful search engine that randomly visits sites on the Web and catalogs them by title, headings, and words in the text. The Lycos search database is one of largest on the Internet. It also provides Internet information services for browsing by category.

Go To Lycos

Using your Web browser, go to the following address: **http://www.lycos.com**

Search for businesses, software, and other areas of the Internet

Click a category to go to a Lycos Internet guide to browse through subcategories and pages of interest

Search the Web, pictures only, sound files, and other specific areas

Type a search phrase and click the Go Get It button

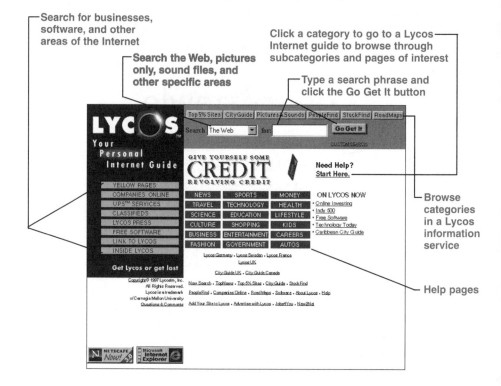

Browse categories in a Lycos information service

Help pages

Search Pages: Metacrawler

Metacrawler sends your search phrase to other search pages, such as Lycos, Infoseek, and many more. Metacrawler queries the search engines and organizes the search results into a systematic list. Searches take longer to perform but are more comprehensive.

Go To Metacrawler

Using your Web browser, go to the following address: **http://www.metacrawler.com**

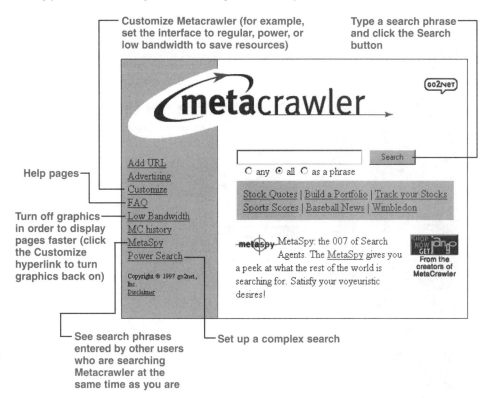

Customize Metacrawler (for example, set the interface to regular, power, or low bandwidth to save resources)

Type a search phrase and click the Search button

Help pages

Turn off graphics in order to display pages faster (click the Customize hyperlink to turn graphics back on)

See search phrases entered by other users who are searching Metacrawler at the same time as you are

Set up a complex search

Search Pages: Switchboard

The Switchboard is a Web page that you can use to find people and businesses on the Internet. Find e-mail addresses and street addresses, including directions on how to get from your house to a particular business.

Go to Switchboard

Using your Web browser, go to the following address: **http://switchboard.com**

Find businesses in your area by category; click the car icon next to the business name to get detailed driving directions from your house to the business

Add yourself to the Switchboard directory

Find individuals

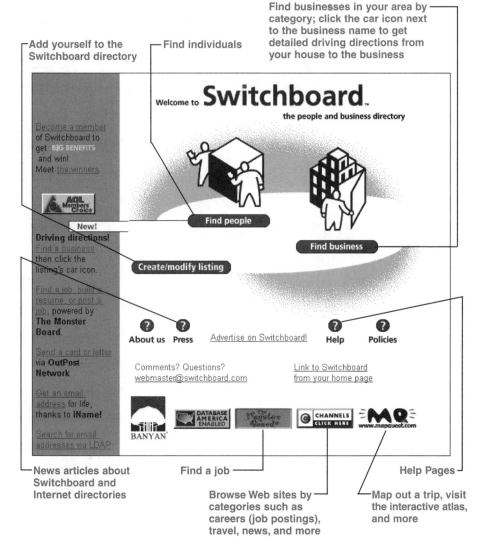

News articles about Switchboard and Internet directories

Find a job

Help Pages

Browse Web sites by categories such as careers (job postings), travel, news, and more

Map out a trip, visit the interactive atlas, and more

NOTE: For more ways to find e-mail addresses, go to the E-mail Address-Finding Tools page on the Web. This page contains a list of hyperlinks to sites that you can use to find e-mail addresses. The address is http://twod.med.harvard.edu/labgc/roth/Emailsearch.html

Search Pages: WebCrawler

This page features "plain English" searching. Enter a descriptive search phrase and WebCrawler finds documents that match any or all of your search terms.

Go To WebCrawler

Using your Web browser, go to the following address: **http://www.webcrawler.com**

Type a search phrase and click the Search button

Customize WebCrawler (for example, set how much detail about each site to include in the search results)

Best sites on the Internet

Weather, news, classifieds, and other sites by category

Amusing facts and sites

Help pages

Search sites in different countries

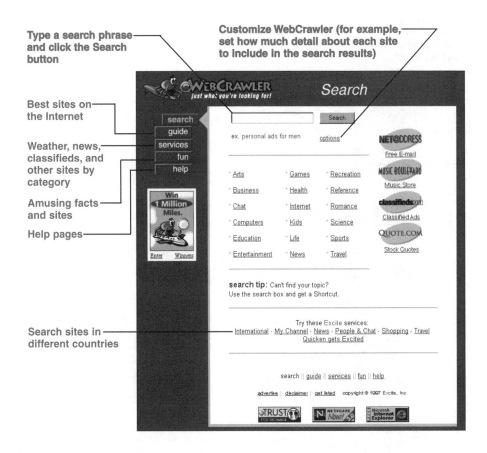

19

Search Pages: Yahoo

Yahoo presents Web topics in well-organized categories that make browsing easy. You can also enter search phrases to search the Yahoo index.

Go to Yahoo

Using your Web browser, go to the following address: **http://www.yahoo.com**

Type a search phrase and click Search to search all categories

Click a round button at the top of the screen to browse new, cool, newsbreaking, and other sites of interest

Set search options (such as searching for e-mail addresses instead of Yahoo categories) and get help on using Yahoo

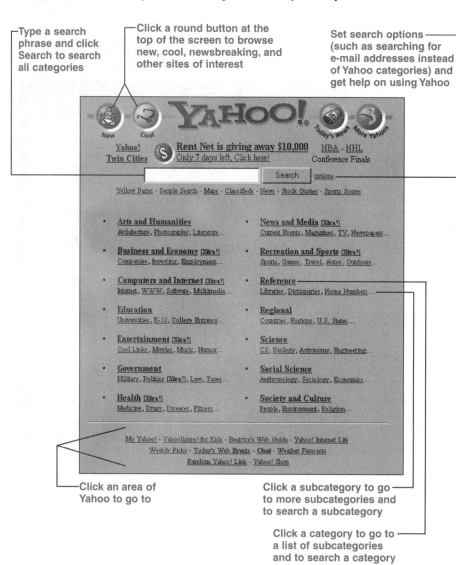

Click an area of Yahoo to go to

Click a subcategory to go to more subcategories and to search a subcategory

Click a category to go to a list of subcategories and to search a category

URL: Internet Site Addresses

Each site on the Internet has an address that identifies it. This address is used to locate the site. This page gives you an overview of Internet addresses, called URLs. URL stands for Uniform Resource Locator.

A URL has several parts:

- The first part of a Web page address is http. This stands for Hypertext Transfer Protocol, which is the protocol used on the Web. A protocol is a set of rules used to exchange information between computers.

- The first part of an FTP address is ftp, which stands for File Transfer Protocol since ftp sites store files that users can download.

- After the protocol type, is a colon and two forward slashes, such as http:// or ftp://.

- Next is the address of the computer on which the site is stored. The computer address is used to identify the computer on the network. For example, www.aol.com is a computer address. For example, http://www.microsoft.com.

- Part of the computer address includes the domain type. This is the three character extension at the end of the computer name. The domain type identifies the type of organization of the host computer. For example, the .com extension stands for a commercial or business organization, such as microsoft.com. The .edu extension identifies an educational facility, such as umich.edu, which is the site for the University of Michigan.

- Some addresses include a path after the computer address and a filename. For example, the address http://www.cio.com/WebMaster/wmlearned.html has a quite a long pathname and also includes the name of a file: wmlearned.html. The file extension "html" stands for Hypertext Markup Language. Sometimes HTML files use the file extension "htm." HTML is file format for a Web page.

- Your Web browser displays the address of the currently-displayed page, usually in the Status bar at the bottom of the screen or in a text box at the top of the screen. When you create a bookmark (called Favorite Places in AOL and Internet Explorer) for a page, the Web browser stores the page address.

- When you type a URL, type it carefully. URLs are case sensitive and have to be entered exactly, so be sure to check for accuracy. If you are using Netscape Communicator or Internet Explorer, you do not have to type the http:// part of the address. Unless you specify otherwise, these browsers assume that you are trying to connect to a Web page.

URL: Internet Site Addresses (continued...)

Enter an Address in AOL

1 Press **Ctrl+K** to open the Keyword window.

2 Type the address and press **Enter**.

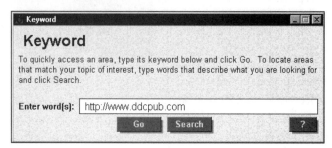

> NOTE: If the Web browser window is open, you can type the address in the address box under the Web browser toolbar.

Enter an Address in Internet Explorer

1 Click the address displayed in the Address box.

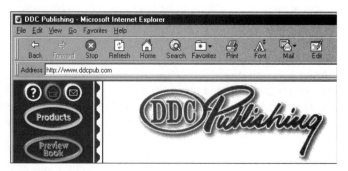

2 Type address of site to go to.

3 Press **Enter**.

Enter an Address in Netscape Communicator

1   Type the address of the site to go to in the **Netsite** text box.

2   Press **Enter**.

America Online

 Started in 1985, America Online has grown into a huge network of services and people. AOL is a global community providing Internet access, online publications, e-mail, hundreds of newsgroups, live interactive forums, and thousands of files and software to download.

With a rapidly growing membership of almost eight million, AOL is far and above the world's largest service provider.

America Online software is free. Each new AOL startup disk comes with 50 free hours of online time. Call America Online at 800-827-6364 for pricing information and to have a startup disk sent to you.

Sign On and Sign Off

Start up AOL and connect to the network. Store your password if you do not want to type it each time you sign off. Disconnect and exit when finished with your America Online session.

Notes:

- The Welcome screen, where you sign on to AOL, is displayed automatically whenever you start the AOL software. If you close the Welcome screen, click **Go To**, **Set Up & Sign On** to redisplay it.

- If you do not want to type your password each time you sign on and your computer is secure, see the **Store Password** procedure on the following page.

- AOL stores two access numbers (phone numbers that you use to dial in if accessing the network through a modem). If you have trouble connecting with an access number, try changing it. See the section called **AOL Access Number**.

- AOL needs to know your screen name and your password. To set up multiple screen names, see the section called **Screen Names**.

Sign On to AOL

1 Double-click the AOL icon on your desktop.

OR

Click the **Start** button on the Windows Taskbar and click **Programs, America Online, AOL & Internet**.

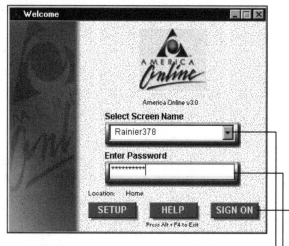

2 Click the drop-down arrow and select a different screen name to use to sign on if desired.

3 Type your password.

4 Click the **SIGN ON** button. AOL connects to the network.

NOTE: If you dial in through a modem, AOL will automatically try the second access number if the first is busy.

- If you store your password, you do not have to type it every time you sign on to AOL. However, anyone with access to your computer can start up AOL and sign on because your password is automatically entered.

- This procedure does not change your password. It only stores it so that you do not have to enter it when you sign on. If you use multiple screen names, you can choose to store a password for any or all names.

Store Password

1 Click **Members**, **Preferences** to open the Preferences window.

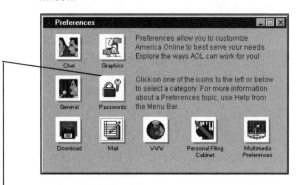

2 Click the **Passwords** button.

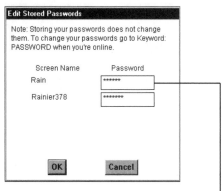

3 Type the password for each screen name that you want to store.

4 Click **OK**.

- If you have an automatic FlashSession scheduled, a confirmation prompt will appear. You need to have your computer on and AOL loaded in order to run an automatic FlashSession. See **Flashsessions**.

Sign Off

Closes all connections to the network and exits AOL.

Click **File**, **Exit**.

AOL Access Number

Your access number is the phone number of the AOL server that you call into to connect to AOL. Use this procedure to change the number.

Notes:

- AOL stores two different access numbers. If the first number is busy or does not answer, it immediately dials the second number when you sign on to America Online.

- If you purchase a new modem at a higher speed, change your access number so that you can connect to a server that is capable of transmitting at the new modem speed.

Change Your Access Number

1 Start up AOL to display the Welcome screen. Do not sign on.

2 Click the drop-down arrow to open the **Select Screen Name** list and click **New Local#**.

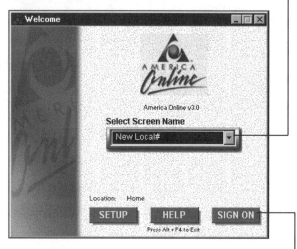

3 Click **SIGN ON**. AOL dials an 800 number. After connecting, a Welcome to America Online screen displays.

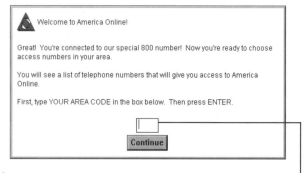

4 Type your area code in the text box.

5 Click **Continue**. A list of access numbers in your area code displays.

Notes:

- If you often get a busy signal when dialing in on your current number(s), it does not hurt to try a different number.

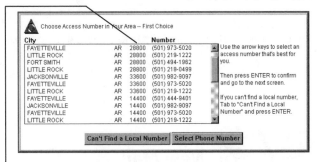

6 Click a location with the correct baud rate for your modem. The baud rate for each access number is listed in the middle column.

*NOTE: If there are no servers in your area, click **Can't Find a Local Number** and enter a different area code.*

7 Click **Select Phone Number**. A second choice list of access numbers displays.

8 Click a second access number to dial if the first number should be busy or does not respond.

9 Click **Select Phone Number**.

10 Click **Continue** to confirm your new access numbers. AOL registers the access numbers and signs off.

AOL Toolbar

Use the AOL toolbar at the top of the America Online window to navigate in AOL. Do not hesitate to click these buttons to explore the network.

 / ***New Mail***

Opens the New Mail window so that you can read new mail messages. When the red flag on the mailbox is up, you have new mail. Click the button to read it. If the flag is down, the button is not activated and you do not have mail. See **E-mail: Read New Mail**.

 Compose Mail

Opens the Compose Mail window so that you can create a new e-mail message. See **E-mail: Create a Mail Message**.

 Channels

Opens the Channels window where you can visit different areas of AOL and the Internet by selecting a category, such as Kids Only or Travel.

 What's Hot

Check out what's new on America Online. The What's Hot window is updated on a regular basis to inform you of new AOL features and includes articles of interest to members. Here you will find contests, information on improvements to channel sites, upcoming live events, and other items.

 People Connection

Takes you to the lobby. From the lobby, you can enter a live chat room and join in on a discussion.

 File Search

Open the Software Search window to search for and browse through AOL's software file archives. Files are available for downloading. See **Download: AOL Software Libraries**.

Stocks & Portfolios

Open the Quotes and Portfolios window to check on the market and get the latest financial news.

 ## Today's News

Read the latest headlines and browse through the news by category. For example, you can go the sports section, check on the weather, and see what is happening in the business world. You can skim the highlights of an article or read it in depth. This site is updated hourly.

 ## World Wide Web

Access the Internet and open your home page. See the **Navigate** sections for more information.

 ## MarketPlace

Shop 24-hours a day in the AOL supermall. Includes links to company Web pages where you can order items online. For example, you can send flowers, order a shirt, and purchase many other products.

 ## My AOL

Customize AOL features to suit your needs. My AOL leads you through the process of setting up preferences, FlashSessions, creating buddy lists, and setting other special preferences.

 ## Online Clock

Click to see how long you have been online during your current AOL session.

 ## Print

Print the e-mail message, newsgroup message, Web page, help topic, or other file that is currently open on your screen. Opens the Print dialog box, where you can select a printer and set the number of copies to print.

AOL Toolbar (continued. . .)

 ## *Personal Filing Cabinet*

Click to open the Personal Filing Cabinet, a storage area on your hard disk where downloaded files, e-mail messages, and newsgroup messages are stored. See **Personal Filing Cabinet**.

 ## *Favorite Places*

Create shortcuts to your favorite Web pages and America Online locations. **See Navigate: Favorite Places**.

 ## *Member Services*

Get help from customer service. Check on your account status, discuss problems with other members, and access other information about using AOL.

 ## *Find*

Search AOL locations to locate people, places, things, and events on America Online. See **Navigate: Search for AOL Locations**.

 ## *Keyword*

Open the Keyword window, where you can type a keyword to go to a particular AOL site. If you know the keyword of an America Online location, use the Keyword button to go directly to the site.

Continue

Download: AOL Software Libraries

Search AOL's extensive library of files for software and other files that you can download. Libraries are packed with shareware (you pay a small fee to register) and freeware (yours for the downloading).

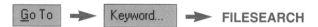 Go To ➡ Keyword... ➡ **FILESEARCH**

Notes:

- Use this procedure to download shareware (you must register and send the author a fee after a trial period) and freeware (no charge). In addition to software, these file libraries include documents on a variety of topics such as tips for video game users, recipes, and an array of other subjects.

- Software for sale is located in an area called the Computing Superstore as described in **Download: Purchase Software**. This page describes the file library containing shareware and freeware.

- When you search for software, you enter keywords, called a search phrase, to define the type of software you are looking for (step 4 in this procedure). Here are some sample search phrases: **graphics** (image files), **software** (drivers, games, utilities, etc.); **video games** (tips on Nintendo and other video games), **recipe** (for cooks), **DTP** (desktop publishing).

Find Free Files

1 Press **Ctrl+K**.

2 Type **filesearch** and press **Enter**.

3 Click the **Download Software** button. The Software Search window opens.

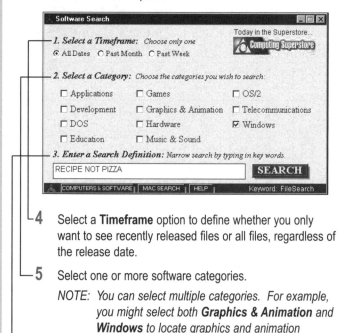

4 Select a **Timeframe** option to define whether you only want to see recently released files or all files, regardless of the release date.

5 Select one or more software categories.

   *NOTE: You can select multiple categories. For example, you might select both **Graphics & Animation** and **Windows** to locate graphics and animation programs developed for Microsoft Windows.*

6 Type a search phrase if desired to further define your search.

   NOTE: You do not have to enter a search phrase. AOL will find files based on categories. However, the list of available files might be so long that it will be difficult to locate exactly what you are looking for.

Notes:

- Use the operators AND, OR, and NOT to define your search. AOL assumes that if you use two or more words in a search phrase they are connected with AND. For example, the search phrase **recipe and pizza** is the same as **recipe pizza**; it finds pizza recipes. Use NOT to exclude topics. For example, **recipe not pizza** finds recipes except for pizza recipes. (The illustration in step 7 shows the files found using this search phrase.) The search phrase **recipes and pizza or seafood** would find only pizza and seafood recipes.

- You can download files immediately or add them to the download list for downloading at a later time using Download Manager or a FlashSession. For more information see **Download: Run Download Manager** and **FlashSessions**.

- Files on AOL servers have been carefully checked for computer viruses. However, you should always use virus-checking software on files downloaded from any location, just to be safe. To acquire virus software, enter the keyword **virus** in the **Search Definition** text box.

7 Click the **Search** button. Files of the type that you specified are listed in the File Search Results window.

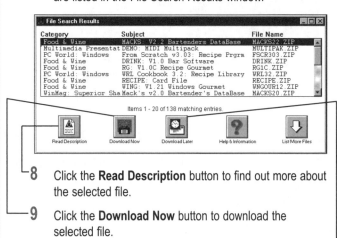

8 Click the **Read Description** button to find out more about the selected file.

9 Click the **Download Now** button to download the selected file.

OR

Click the **Download Later** button to add the selected file to your download list.

NOTE: The download list is the list of files that you will download at a later time. Each time you click the **Download Later** *button, another file is added to the download list. For more information, see* **Download: Download List**.

Download: Download List

The download list is a list of files waiting to be downloaded. The files in the list will be downloaded during the next FlashSession or Download Manager session.

File ➡ Personal Filing Cabinet

Notes:

- Files that are queued for downloading and files that have already been downloaded are stored and listed in the Personal Filing Cabinet. This information is stored in the Files to Download and the Files You've Downloaded subfolders in the Download Manager folder, as shown in the illustration.

- Use this procedure to view the files in the download list. Files are listed chronologically by download date.

Open the Download List

1 Click **File**, **Personal Filing Cabinet** to open the Personal Filing Cabinet window.

NOTE: You can only open the Personal Filing Cabinet if you have files stored there.

2 Double-click the **Download Manager** folder to open it.

3 Double-click the **Files to Download** folder to open it.

Notes:

- Download an individual file in the list. You must be online to download the file.

Download a File in the Download List

1 Follow **Open the Download List** procedure.

2 Right-click the file to download and click **Download**.

3 Select the destination folder and/or change the filename in the Download Manager dialog box.

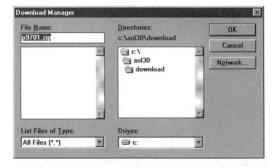

36

4   Click 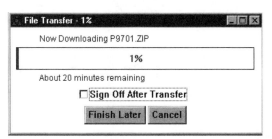 . Download Manager starts downloading the file and displays the File Transfer progress indicator.

File Transfer - 1%
Now Downloading P9701.ZIP
1%
About 20 minutes remaining
☐ Sign Off After Transfer
Finish Later Cancel

5   Click the **Sign Off After Transfer** to automatically exit and disconnect after the file is transferred if desired.

Remove a File from the Download List

1   Follow **Open the Download List** procedure.

2   Right-click the file to delete and click **Delete**.

3   Click [_Yes_] at the confirmation prompt.

Change the Download Destination Folder

1   Follow **Open the Download List** procedure.

2   Right-click the **Files to Download** folder and click **Select Destination**.

3   Double-click the desired destination folder.

4   Click [_Save_] .

Download: Purchase Software

Purchase the latest software and guide books online without leaving your office. America Online offers the atOnce Software online shop.

   Go To ➡ Keyword... ➡ **ATONCE**

Notes:

- You can locate software in one of two ways: browse through categories or enter a search phrase.

- If you choose to enter a search phrase, use keywords to define the kind of software you are looking for. For example, you might type **Microsoft Office** or **fonts** or **virus**. You can use the AND, OR, and NOT operators. For example, you could search for **windows and graphics** (finds only graphics that you can use in Microsoft Windows programs) or **images not mac** (finds pictures that you can use in Microsoft Windows or DOS but not the Macintosh) or **books or guides** (finds all listings for "books" and all listings for "guides").

- You cannot download these files later using a FlashSession or Download Manager. You must download at the time of purchase. Have your credit card handy.

Shop for Software

1 Press **Ctrl+K**.

2 Type **atonce** and press **Enter**.

3 Click the **Instant Software Here** button to open the atOnce Software window.

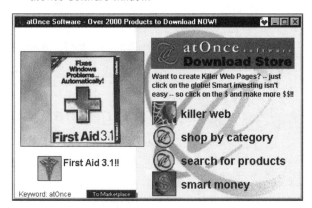

4 Click the **shop by category** button to browse through titles. Categories include games, web, utilities, screensavers, and finance among others. Screens are self-explanatory. Click the category to browse.

OR

a. Click the **search for products** button to enter a search phrase to locate software.

b. Type a search phrase describing the type of software to locate.

c. Click **List Articles**. Products matching the search phrase that you entered appear in the bottom pane of the window.

d. Double-click an item to view information on the product.

5 Click the **Download Now** button to order.

Download: Run Download Manager

Downloading a file copies it to your hard disk. Run Download Manager to copy over the files that you have sent to the queue for later downloading.

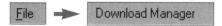

Notes:

- This procedure downloads files in the download list. You add files to the download list by clicking the **Download Later** button at screens where you can download files.

- For more information about the list and about downloading an individual file rather than all of the files, see **Download: Download List**.

- Another way to download the files in the download list is to activate a FlashSession. During a FlashSession, you can upload and download messages in addition to files. See **FlashSessions**.

- The length of time it takes to download depends on the size of the files that you are downloading and the speed of your modem. To see the approximate time that it will take to download a selected file, click the **View Description** button in the Download Manager window. This button is only available if you are working online.

Download Files

1 Click **File**, **Download Manager** to open the Download Manager window.

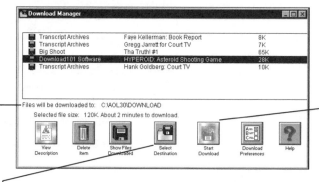

2 To change the destination folder where the files will be downloaded if desired:

a. Click the **Select Destination** button.

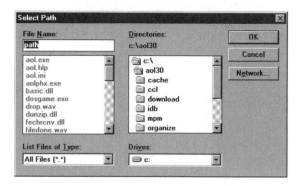

b. Display the desired destination folder in the Select Path dialog box.

c. Click [OK].

NOTE: *This sets the destination folder for future sessions. The current download location is shown in the Download Manager window.*

3 Click the **Start Download** button.

Resume an Interrupted Download

1 Sign on to AOL to reconnect.

2 Click <u>F</u>ile, **Personal Filing Cabinet**.

3 Double-click the **Files to Download** folder to open it.

4 Right-click the interrupted file and click **Download**. The download process resumes where it left off.

Find a Downloaded File

1 Click <u>F</u>ile, **Download Manager**.

2 Click the **Show Files Downloaded** button. The Files You've Downloaded window displays.

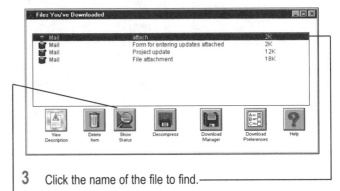

3 Click the name of the file to find.

4 Click **Show Status**.

Download: Set Download Preferences

Customize the downloading process. Settings apply to downloading with both FlashSessions and Download Manager.

Notes:

• Set a variety of options to customize downloading, such as how to handle compressed (ZIP) files.

Set Download Preferences

1 Click **Members**, **Preferences**.

2 Click the **Download** button to open the Download Preferences window.

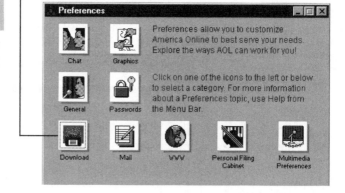

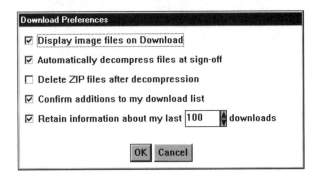

3   Set options as follows:

- **Display image files on Download.** If downloading avi, art, jpg, bmp, or gif graphics files, displays the image while downloading the file. It takes longer to download graphics if you display them.

- **Automatically decompress files at sign-off.** Files that you download from the AOL Software area are compressed so that they take up less disk space and download faster. If you check this option, these files are automatically decompressed for you.

- **Delete ZIP files after decompression.** Deletes the compressed file after decompressing it to save disk space. Saves the original, decompressed file and removes the compressed file.

- **Confirm additions to my download list.** Displays a message each time you click the **Download Later** button. The message confirms that the file was added to the list of files to download.

- **Retain information about my downloads.** Sets the number of files (up to 1,000) to list in the Files You've Downloaded list in Download Manager and the Personal Filing Cabinet.

4   Click OK.

E-Mail: Address Book

Store the names and e-mail addresses of companies and individuals with whom you exchange mail. When you create a mail message, simply select recipient name(s) from the address book.

- Add e-mail addresses to your address book so that you can quickly address mail messages by selecting recipient(s).

- When you add an AOL member to your address book, you need only enter their screen name. An AOL screen name is also the e-mail name. For example, if your screen name is X189, your e-mail name is X189.

- You can enter multiple names in a single address book entry if you often send the same mail to a number of people. For example, you could create an entry with a name such as Book Club and enter the e-mail addresses of the members of the club.

- You can use this procedure to modify existing entries in your address book. Select a name in the address book (shown in step 1) and click the **Modify** button.

Create Address Book Entries

1 Click **Mail**, **Edit Address Book** to open the address book.

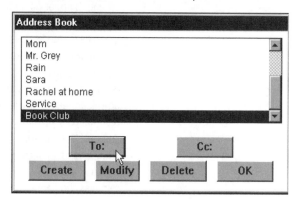

2 Click **Create** to open the Address Group dialog box.

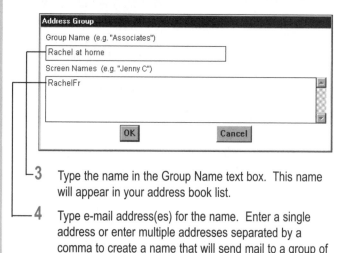

3 Type the name in the Group Name text box. This name will appear in your address book list.

4 Type e-mail address(es) for the name. Enter a single address or enter multiple addresses separated by a comma to create a name that will send mail to a group of recipients.

5 Click **OK**.

Notes:

- Mail addressed to non-AOL users is sent over the Internet. You need to enter Internet e-mail address information as follows: e-mail name, @ sign, domain name. For example, you might send mail to *name@msn.com* (a Microsoft Network user) or *name@compuserve.com* (a CompuServe user). If a non-AOL user sends you mail, the sender must also include Internet e-mail information. They would send mail to *X189@aol.com* (if X189 is your e-mail name). The *aol.com* segment of the Internet address identifies the domain (America Online) so that mail can be routed to your mail server from other domains.

- To enter multiple recipients, separate each name with a comma. For example: *RachelFr, name@compuserve.com, name@msn.com*

6   Repeat from step 2 if desired to add more address book entries.

7   Click OK to close the Address Book dialog box when finished.

Delete an Address Book Entry

By removing names of people with whom you no longer correspond, you can more quickly find addresses when creating messages.

1   Click **Mail**, **Edit Address Book** to open the address book.

2   Click the name to delete.

3   Click Delete .

4   Click OK to close the Address Book dialog box when finished.

E-Mail: Create a Mail Message

Create an e-mail message. Address the mail by selecting e-mail names and addresses from your address book.

Mail ➡ Compose Mail

Notes:

- Choose from two types of recipients for your message when selecting names from the address book: TO recipients and CC recipients. TO recipients are the main people for whom the message is intended. You must enter at least one TO recipient in a mail message. CC recipients are other people who might be interested in the message. CC recipients are called "carbon copy recipients" or "courtesy copy recipients."

- You can also send a copy of your message to a BCC (blind carbon copy) recipient. The name of this type of recipient does not appear anywhere in the message. To add a BCC recipient, type the e-mail address enclosed in parentheses in either the TO or the CC box. The name will not be visible to other recipients. Example: (*Sheila@gte.net*)

Create a Mail Message

To place a hyperlink to one of your favorite places in a mail message, click **Go To**, **Favorite Places**. Drag the icon for the favorite place from the menu to the body of the mail message. The recipient can click on the hyperlink to open the Web page.

You can search for a pen pal who shares your interests. Press **Ctrl+K** and type **pen pals** to find people from around the world who are looking for pen pals who want to exchange e-mail.

1 Press **Ctrl+M** to create a new mail message.

2 To enter message recipient(s) by selecting them from the address book:

a. Click Address Book . The Address Book window displays.

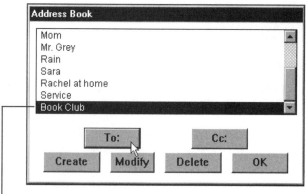

b. Click the recipient name.

NOTE: To move quickly to a name in the address book, type the first letter of the name.

c. Click To: to add the address of a main recipient

or click Cc: to add a carbon copy recipient. Repeat as necessary to enter recipients.

d. Click OK to return to the Compose Mail screen. Recipient(s) are added to the message.

3 Type a title in the Subject text box.

4 Type the body of the message.

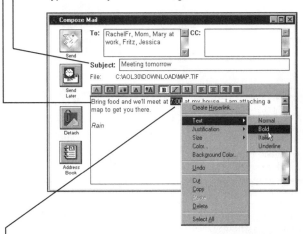

5 To format text in the body of the message if desired:

a. Drag over text to format.

b. Right-click to open shortcut menu.

c. Set formatting options as desired.

6 Click Send to send the message immediately.

OR

Click Send Later to send the message at the next FlashSession.

7 Click OK at the prompt.

Edit Unsent Mail

Open and edit mail that has been created but not yet sent. This procedure is only available if you clicked the **Send Later** button when you created the message to send it in the next FlashSession.

1 Click **Mail**, **Read Outgoing Flash Mail**.

2 Double-click the message to edit.

3 Click ☒ to close the message and save changes.

E-Mail: File Attachments

Send a file by attaching it to an e-mail message and download file attachments that you receive through mail. Downloading copies the file to your hard disk.

Attach

Notes:

- If sending a large file, you might want to compress it first. Compressed files are sent and received much more quickly than uncompressed files. The recipient must have compatible file compression software in order to expand the file after receiving it. To find file compression utilities, see **Download: AOL Software Libraries**. Use a keyword such as **file compression** in your search phrase.

- If you use a file compression utility such as WinZip or PKZIP, you can compress multiple files into a single file. That way, you can send multiple files in a single mail message. Otherwise, you must send each individual file in a separate mail message.

- Files sent through Internet mail to non-AOL members are encoded in MIME format. The mail software that the recipient is using must be able to decode MIME files.

Attach a File to a Mail Message

1 Create the message to which you will attach the file.

   *NOTE: See **E-Mail: Create a Mail Message**.*

2 Click .

3 Select the file's drive and folder location from the **Look in** drop-down list.

4 Double-click the file to attach in the Attach File dialog box.

   The filename is added to the mail message.

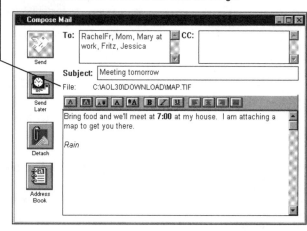

NOTE: To remove a file attachment, click Detach .

5 Send the mail message.

Download a File Received in a Mail Message

1 Open the message.

NOTE: To go to the New Mail window and open new messages, see E-Mail: Read New Messages.

2 Click $\boxed{\text{Download Later}}$ to add the file to the download list for later downloading using a FlashSession or Download Manager. Click $\boxed{\text{OK}}$ at the prompt.

OR

- To download the file now:

a. Click $\boxed{\text{Download File}}$.

b. Change the download location and/or filename in the Download Manager dialog box if desired.

c. Click $\boxed{\text{Save}}$. A File Transfer indicator displays.

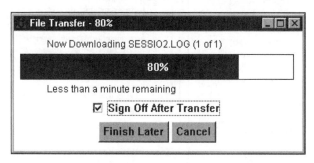

d. Click **Sign off after transfer** if you want to automatically disconnect and exit when the transfer is complete.

NOTE: While the file is downloading, you can switch to other windows and continue to work online as AOL downloads in the background. When the download is complete, the File Transfer indicator closes. In addition, the message "File's done" sounds if your computer is equipped for sound.

E-Mail: Find AOL Members

Use the Member Directory to locate America Online users. Create your member profile if you wish to be included in the Member Directory.

Members ➡ Member Directory

Notes:

- The AOL Member Directory lists AOL members who have created a member profile. Each screen name has a different profile.

- To find a member, you can search for their screen name, interests and hobbies, city, or any other information stored in member profiles. However, members have control over what they enter in the profile and they might not have included, for example, their city or their name. Only members who have filled out a member profile are listed in the directory.

- You can create or edit your member profile from the Member Directory dialog box. Click the **My Profile** button.

- To find non-AOL members, you can search directories on the Internet to locate the e-mail addresses of individuals and businesses. Press **Ctrl+F** and double-click **Switchboard** in the Places and Things tab.

Search the AOL Member Directory

1   Click **Members**, **Member Directory** to open the Member Directory window.

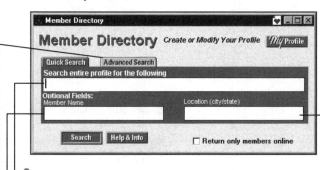

2   Type the text you will use to locate the member. This can be any information from any field in a profile. You must type something in this field.

3   Type the member name if you know it, if desired. Keep in mind that the member name is not necessarily the screen name of the person you are looking for.

    *NOTE: AOL members can use any name they want for a screen name. In fact, you can have up to five screen names for one member (see the **Screen Names** section) and none of these names have to be their real name. A member might add their real name to the AOL Member Directory. Thus, you would not be able to find them by searching for a screen name. Or, if the member added a screen name to the directory, you would be unable to find them by searching for their real name.*

4   Type a location if desired.

5   Click the **Advanced Search** tab to enter more profile information to search for if desired.

6   Click **Search** .

Find a Member Who is Currently Online

1 Press **Ctrl+L** to open the Locate Member Online window.

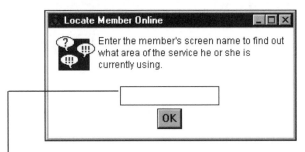

2 Type the member's screen name and press **Enter**.

Send an Instant Message

Send a message to a member who is currently online. If the recipient is not online, the message will not go through.

1 Press **Ctrl+I**.

2 Type the recipient's screen name and a brief message.

3 Click **Send**.

Create or Edit Your Member Profile

If you use multiple screen names, each screen name has a different member profile. In order to create or edit the profile for a particular screen name, you must sign on to AOL using that name.

1 Click **Members**, **Member Directory**.

2 Click **My Profile**.

3 Fill in information about yourself as desired.

4 Click **Update**.

E-Mail: Read New Mail

Part of the fun of AOL is getting your new messages. Use these procedures to read new mail messages either online or after retrieving them in a FlashSession.

Mail ➡ Read New Mail

Notes:

- When you have new mail, the red flag on the mail button (in the AOL toolbar) is in the up position:

  . You can click this button to read mail.

- To reply to a message you have received or to forward it to another person, see **E-Mail: Reply to and Forward Mail Messages**.

- If you receive unsolicited junk mail, forward it to the TOSspam e-mail name. That way, AOL can prevent users from flooding mailboxes with unwanted mail.

- To mark a message as unread even if you have read it, click the **Keep as New** button. Since a FlashSession downloads only unread mail, you can use this button to download messages in the next FlashSession even after reading them.

- If you click the **Ignore** button in the New Mail window, the message is marked as read even if you do not read it.

Read New Mail Online

1   Press **Ctrl+R**. If you have any new mail, the New Mail window displays.

NOTE: The New Mail window shows only those messages addressed to the e-mail name that you used to sign on to AOL during the current session. To see mail addressed to a different screen name, you must sign on to AOL using that name.

2   Double-click the message to read. The message opens in a separate window.

NOTE: AOL deletes unread messages after 27 days. AOL deletes messages that you have read after about three to five days. (Marking a message using the **Keep As New** button does not change this.) To access your messages later, you need to save them. To automatically save all messages that you receive, see **E-Mail: Set Mail Preferences**. To save an individual message, see **Save a Mail Message** in this section. If you retrieve your mail with a FlashSession, new mail is automatically copied to your hard disk.

Notes:

- Messages that you have read are removed from the New Mail window. Until they are deleted, you can use this procedure to open them.

Open Previously Read Messages Online

Click **Mail**, **Check Mail You've Read**.

Notes:

- After downloading, use this procedure to open your new mail.

- To respond to a message, see **E-Mail: Reply to and Forward Mail Messages**.

Read Mail Downloaded in a FlashSession

1   Click **Mail**, **Read Incoming Mail**.

2   Double-click the message to read.

Notes:

- Specify the file type when you save (such as a text file).

- To automatically save all new messages, see **E-mail: Set Mail Preferences**.

Save a Mail Message

Save a message in a separate file where you can later open it with your word processor.

1   Open the message to save.

2   Press **Ctrl+S**.

3   Type a file name for the message in the Save As dialog box.

   NOTE: The mail is saved in the AOL Download folder unless you designate a different folder before saving.

4   Click [**Save**].

E-Mail: Reminder Messages

Have AOL send you reminders in advance of important holidays and events.
For example, set up a reminder for a friend's birthday, an anniversary, or other event.

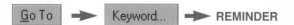 Go To → Keyword... → REMINDER

Notes:

- You will receive your e-mail reminder message 14 days before the specified event. You can request that a second reminder be sent four days before the event.

Add a Reminder

1 Press **Ctrl+K**.

2 Type **reminder** in the Keyword dialog box and press **Enter**. The Reminder Service window opens.

3 Click the graphic next to **Create Your Reminder** to open the Enter Your Reminders Here window.

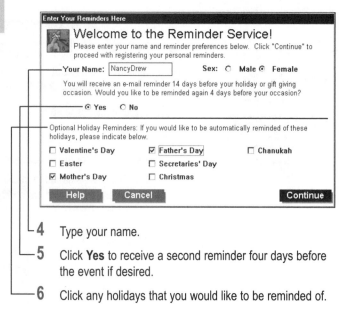

4 Type your name.

5 Click **Yes** to receive a second reminder four days before the event if desired.

6 Click any holidays that you would like to be reminded of.

7 Click the **Continue** button. The Add a Reminder Here window opens.

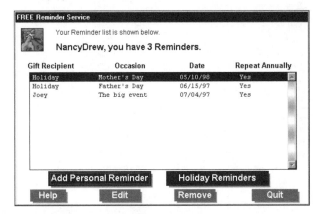

8 Enter information about the event and click **Save** when finished. A list of the reminders that you have created is displayed.

FREE Reminder Service

Your Reminder list is shown below.

NancyDrew, you have 3 Reminders.

Gift Recipient	Occasion	Date	Repeat Annually
Holiday	Mother's Day	05/10/98	Yes
Holiday	Father's Day	06/15/97	Yes
Joey	The big event	07/04/97	Yes

Add Personal Reminder   Holiday Reminders

Help   Edit   Remove   Quit

9 To add more reminders if desired, click **Add Personal Reminder** (opens the Add a Reminder Here window as shown above) or **Holiday Reminders** (allows you to add more holidays from the preset list of holidays provided by AOL).

10 When finished, click **Quit**.

E-Mail: Reply to and Forward Mail Messages

Reply to the sender (or the sender and all recipients) of an e-mail message that you have received. Or, send a message that you have received to another recipient.

 / /

Reply to a Mail Message

1 Display the message to reply to.

2 Select the text in the message that you want to include in the reply if desired.

3 Click ![Reply] to reply to the sender of the message only.

OR

Click ![Reply to All] to reply to the sender and send a copy of the message to all other recipients of the original message.

4 Type your message in the message body.

- The TO recipient is filled in for you with the name of the sender of the original message.

- The Subject field is filled in with the original subject with Re: added to show that this is a reply.

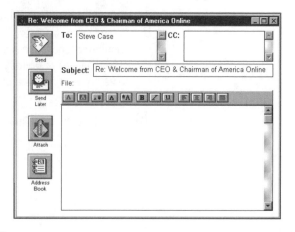

5 Format message text if desired (see procedure on next page).

6 Send the message (see procedure on next page).

Notes:

- The Subject line is filled in for you, using the subject of the original message with the characters Fw: added to let the recipient know that this is a forwarded message.

- The text of the original message that you are forwarding is set off using special characters. That way, the recipient can easily see which part of the message is the original and which part is your message. AOL places the characters << at the beginning of the original message and >> at the end. Original text in mail forwarded to you over the Internet by non-AOL users is set off with a single > at the beginning of each line.

Notes:

- You can only format the body of a message. You cannot format recipient or subject text.

Notes:

- You can send the message immediately if you are working online. Or, work offline and send all the messages that you have created in a single FlashSession. FlashSessions are quick and easy to set up and can save you time. For more information, see **FlashSessions**.

Forward a Mail Message

Forwarding a message sends a copy of a message that you receive to someone else. You can add your own message in a forwarded message.

1   Display the message to forward. (See **E-Mail: Read New Mail** for help.)

2   Click Forward.

3   Type your message.

   NOTE: The text of the original message does not appear in the message. However, it will be sent in the forwarded message.

4   Format message text if desired (see procedure below).

5   Send the message (see procedure below).

   *NOTE: If you want to save a copy of all messages that you send, see **E-Mail: Mail Preferences**. Saved messages are stored in the Personal Filing Cabinet.*

Format Mail Message Text

1   Drag over text to select the text to format.

2   Click a formatting button on the toolbar above the message body:

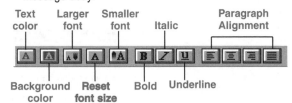

Send a Mail Message

Click Send to send the message immediately.

OR

Click Send Later to send the message in the next FlashSession.

57

E-Mail: Set Mail Preferences

Set mail preferences to customize how your mail works. For example, you can automatically save copies of all messages that you send and receive.

Mem**b**ers ➡ Preferences

Notes:

- AOL deletes messages that you receive about three to five days after you read them. To save copies of all messages that you receive, mark the **Retain all mail I read** preference. To save copies of all messages that you send, mark the **Retain all mail I send** preference. By default, AOL does not save messages. Messages that you save are stored in your Personal Filing Cabinet in the Mail folder. See **Personal Filing Cabinet**. If you retrieve mail with a FlashSession, incoming mail is copied to your hard disk.

Set Mail Preferences

1 Click **Mem**b**ers**, **Preferences** to open the Preferences dialog box.

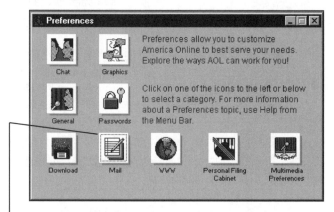

2 Click the **Mail** button to open the Mail Preferences dialog box.

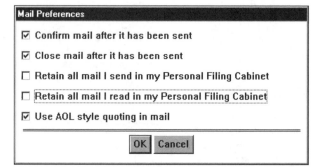

3 Set mail preferences as follows:

• **Confirm mail after it has been sent**. When selected, you will hear "Mail sent" or see the message when you send mail. If cleared, the message is disabled.

• **Close mail after it has been sent.** Closes the Compose Mail window after you send a message. If cleared, the window remains open on the screen and you click ⊠ to close it.

• **Retain all mail I send in my Personal Filing Cabinet**. Saves a copy of all messages that you send. Stores the copies in the Personal Filing Cabinet.

• **Retain all mail I read in my Personal Filing Cabinet**. Saves a copy of all messages that you receive. Stores the copies in the Personal Filing Cabinet.

• **Use AOL style quoting in mail**. Specifies how AOL marks original text in messages that you forward and reply to. By default, it surrounds the original message in chevrons: <<message>>. Clear the preference if you want to use Internet quoting, which adds > to the beginning of each line of text in the original message.

4 Click OK .

5 Click ⊠ to close the Preferences dialog box.

FlashSessions

Run a FlashSession to download and upload e-mail, newsgroup messages, and files. Schedule automated FlashSessions to run unattended at any time.

Mail ➡ Set Up FlashSession...

Notes:

- Typically, users run a FlashSession just before exiting AOL to wrap up a session. Follow the **Set Up a FlashSession** procedure to specify the tasks to run.

- If you choose the **Download selected files** task, the FlashSession retrieves the files in the download list (files queued for later downloading). See **Download Manager: Download List** for more information.

- When you activate the session you can specify that AOL automatically sign off after performing all tasks.

- If you store your password, you can use this procedure while working offline. When you activate a FlashSession while working offline, it signs on to AOL for you. To store passwords, follow steps 1 through 4 in the **Schedule Automated FlashSessions** procedure on the next page.

Set Up a FlashSession

A FlashSession quickly performs tasks that you specify, such as retrieving new e-mail and newsgroup messages, sending messages that you created offline, downloading files, and other tasks.

Set up a FlashSession to specify which tasks AOL will perform during the next FlashSession. These settings are retained so that each time a FlashSession runs, the tasks specified here are performed.

1 Click **Mail**, **Set Up FlashSession** to open the FlashSessions window.

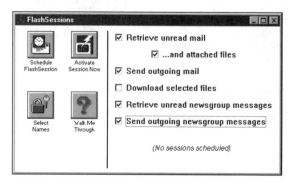

2 Select tasks to perform in the next FlashSession.

*NOTE: You can download files marked for later downloading during a FlashSession or you can run Download Manager. See **Download: Run Download Manager**.*

3 Click ☒ to close the window and save the settings for the next FlashSession.

Activate a FlashSession

1 Click **Mail**, **Activate FlashSession Now**.

2 Click **Sign off when finished** to have AOL automatically sign off and exit when the session is finished, if desired.

NOTE: To change the tasks that are set up for FlashSessions, click the **Set Session** button.

3 Click **Begin**.

Schedule Automated FlashSessions

Run unattended FlashSessions at your convenience. For example, you can schedule a Flash-Session to run while you are asleep or away from your computer.

1 Click **Mail**, **Set Up FlashSession**.

2 Click the **Select Names** button.

3 Click the screen name and type the corresponding password to use to sign on for the session.

4 Click **OK**. You are returned to the FlashSessions window.

5 Click the **Schedule FlashSession** button.

6 Click **Enable Scheduler** to select it.

NOTE: The Scheduler is disabled by default. You can disable it any time you want to skip scheduled sessions. Scheduled FlashSessions will not run unless this option is selected.

7 Set options to determine how often and at what time to run automated FlashSessions.

NOTE: For example, you could schedule a FlashSession to run every Sunday starting at 7am and running again every two hours throughout the day.

8 Click **OK**.

FTP Servers

FTP servers store files that you can download. AOL has placed a list of favorite FTP servers that you can browse. This makes it easier to locate an FTP server.

Go To ➡ Keyword... ➡ FTP

Notes:

- Downloading a file copies the file from a server to your hard disk. FTP (File Transfer Protocol) is the Internet standard for copying files between computers.

- If you are looking for software to download, see **Download: AOL Software Libaries** and **Download: Purchase Software**. See also **Shareware.com**. These are much easier places to find software than on FTP servers. Areas on the Internet such as Web pages where you can download files use FTP but are much easier to work with than an FTP server.

- Anonymous FTP means that you do not need a password or other special access right in order to connect to the server.

Download a File from an FTP Site

1   Press **Ctrl+K** to open the Keyword window.

2   Type **FTP** and press **Enter** to display the FTP window.

NOTE: For help on using FTP in AOL, read the information in the list of folders.

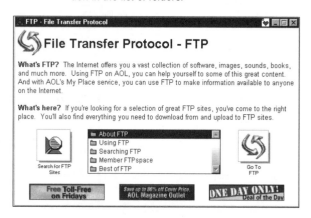

3   Click the **Go To FTP** button to open the Anonymous FTP window.

62

4   Scroll through the list of sites and double-click the site to open. The following illustration shows the Microsoft FTP site.

   *NOTE: Click the **Other Site** button if you know the address of an FTP server and want to connect to it.*

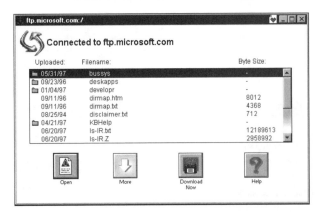

5   To work with FTP files:
   - Double-click a folder to open until the file you want to download is displayed.
   - Double-click a file to see a description of the file.
   - Click the file to download and click the **Download Now** button.

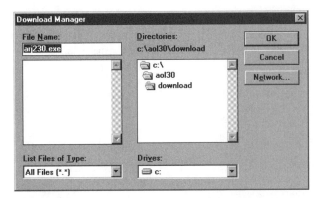

   - Set the file name and directory in the Download Manager window and click **Ok** to download.

6   Click ⊠ to close window when finished.

Log a Session

Keep a record of sites that you visit during a session and/or chats that you participate in. You can also log the text of instant messages sent and received.

File ➡ Log Manager

Notes:

- Log your activities in AOL in two separate logs: the *chat log* and the *session log*.

- Open a session log to record text in the sites you visit. Text that appears in scrolling text boxes on any screen that you display is saved in the session log. For example, if you visit a news site and open an article, the text in the article is saved in the log. The session log can also record instant messages.

- You can either create a new log file for the current session or you can append the information to the end of an existing log file.

- Open a chat log to record conversations you have in chat rooms.

- By default, the name of the session log file is *session.log* and the name of the chat log is *chat.log*. You can change the log file name whenever you start logging. Make sure that the file has a .log extension.

Start a Log File

1   Click **File**, **Log Manager**. The Logging dialog box displays.

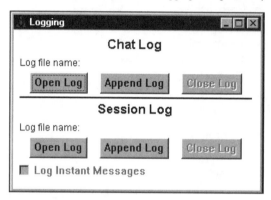

2   To append the log for the current AOL session to the end of an existing log file if desired:

   a. Click **Append Log** located under the Session Log or Chat Log section, depending on which type of information you are recording.

   b. Double-click the existing file to which the new log will be added.

3   To create a new log for the current session if desired:

   a. Click the **Open Log** under the Session Log or Chat Log section, depending on which type of information you would like to record.

64

The Open Log dialog box displays. This illustration shows the dialog box for a chat log.

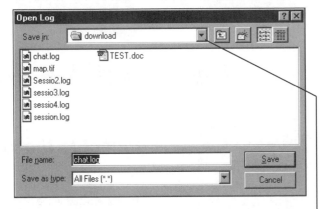

b. Click **Save in** and select a different directory in which to store the log if desired.

NOTE: Depending on your system configuration, the directory structure might be displayed in the Open Log dialog box on the right side of the screen.

c. Click ___Save___.

NOTE: Depending on your system configuration, the Open Log dialog box might have an OK button rather than a Save button.

4 Repeat step 2 or 3 to start another log if desired.

5 Click **Log instant messages** if desired to include instant messages in a session log.

NOTE: This option is available only if you started a session log.

6 Click ☒ to close the window.

Stop Logging

1 Click **File**, **Log Manager**.

2 Click **Close Log** located under the log that you would like to stop.

3 Click ☒ to close the window.

Navigate: Connect to the Internet

Connect directly to the Web by opening your home page or go through the Internet Connection window where you can browse Internet sites by category.

Go To ➡ Keyword... ➡ **WWW or INTERNET**

Notes:

- To connect to the Web, you must be using version 3.0 of the AOL software (PC) or version 2.7 (Macintosh). To upgrade, open the Keyword window (**Ctrl+K**) and type **upgrade**.

Connect to the Web

- Click [image] in the AOL toolbar.

OR

- Press **Ctrl+K**. Type **www** in the Keyword window and press **Enter**.

Connecting to the Internet using this procedure opens your Web home page. By default, this is the AOL home page. For more information, see **Navigate: Home Page**.

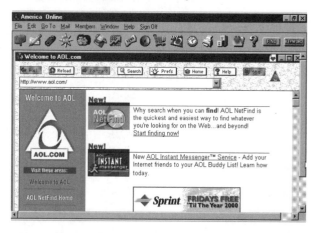

To begin searching the web:

    a. Click [🔍 Search] to display your Internet Search page.

    b. Enter a search topic and press **Enter**. See **Navigate: Internet Search Page** for more details.

Notes:

- Another way to connect to the Internet is through an AOL channel. If you browse through or search for topics in a channel, and the item that you select is a Web page, the AOL Web browser automatically starts and displays the page.

- You can connect to the Internet by adding web sites to the Favorite Places toolbar button and menu item. Selecting a favorite place takes you to the specified Web page or other site. See **Navigate: Favorite Places**.

- The Internet Connection window is an AOL (not an Internet) site. When you connect to a location on the Internet, the Web browser starts. For a description of the browser window and toolbar buttons, see **Navigate: Web Browser**.

- To connect to the Web, you must be using version 3.0 of the AOL software (PC) or version 2.7 (Macintosh). To upgrade, open the Keyword window (**Ctrl+K**) and type **upgrade**.

Connect to the Internet Through Internet Connection

AOL provides the Internet Connection, from which you can access Web pages, Gopher sites, FTP servers, and a wealth of information on AOL and the Internet.

1 Press **Ctrl+K** to open the Keyword window.

2 Type **internet** and press **Enter**. The Internet Connection window displays.

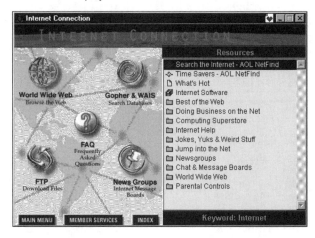

3 To go to a site:

- Click a button in the left pane to connect to an area of the Internet.

- Double-click an item in the right pane to get more information about using the Internet through AOL and to access specific sites, such as sites where you can download software or favorite member sites.

Navigate: Disable Graphics on Web Pages

If speed is more important to you than viewing graphics, opening a Web page is much faster if you turn off the graphic display. Use this procedure to view text only or to include both text and graphics on Web pages.

Notes:

- If AOL does not have to load graphics when opening Web pages, the pages will display much faster. Part of the fun of exploring the Internet is the graphic elements on Web pages, but they can really slow you down. When you want to quickly find information, disable graphics.

- When graphics are disabled, graphics on Web pages are replaced by text placeholders.

- You can also choose whether or not to display compressed graphics (applies only when graphics are enabled). Compressed graphics can download faster with a slight reduction in the quality of the picture. By default, AOL displays compressed graphics.

- You can perform this procedure while you are working offline or online.

Enable or Disable Graphics

1 Click **Members**, **Preferences** to open the Preferences window.

2 Click to open the AOL Internet Properties dialog box.

NOTE: *If you are online, you can click* 🔅 **Prefs** *on the browser toolbar.*

NOTE: *Depending on your system configuration, the WWW Preferences dialog box might display instead of the AOL Internet Properties dialog box.*

3 Click the General tab.

4 Click **Show pictures** to mark or clear the check box. When marked, graphics are enabled.

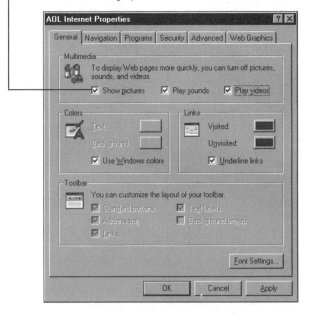

- If you enable/disable graphics when you have a Web page displayed, click

  [🔁 Reload] to apply the new setting to the page. You might do this, for example, if you enable graphics to see the graphics on the current page.

NOTE: *You can also enable/disable sounds and videos using the **Play sounds** and **Play videos** options.*

NOTE: *If the WWW Preferences dialog box is displayed, clear the **No Graphics** option to disable graphics.*

5 To set graphic compression on/off if desired:

NOTE: *If the WWW Preferences dialog box is displayed, use the Compressed Graphics and Uncompressed Graphics options as desired.*

a. Click the **Web Graphics** tab.

b. Click **Use Compressed Graphics** to mark or clear the check box. When the option is marked, graphics are compressed and display faster at the expense of quality.

6 Click [OK].

View a Graphic in Text-Only Mode

Use this procedure to view an individual graphic on a page when graphics are disabled.

1 Right-click the graphic placeholder.

2 Click **Show Picture**.

Navigate: Favorite Places

Create shortcuts to your favorite Internet and America Online sites so that you can revisit them with a click of the mouse button.

Go To ➡ Favorite Places

Notes:

• After you create a shortcut to a favorite place, you can go directly to it by selecting the name of the site from the Favorite Places menu item or toolbar button.

• Create favorites to both Internet sites (such as Web pages) and to America Online sites.

Add a Site to Favorites

• If the site is displayed on the screen, drag the heart icon (located in the window title of the site) up to the Favorite Places button on the AOL toolbar. When the heart icon is positioned over the Favorite Places button, release the mouse button.

• Click **Window, Add to Favorite Places** if the Web browser window is maximized and the Favorite Places icon is not visible.

• If you know the site address, click **Go To, Favorite Places** and click the **Add Favorite Place** button. Type the address and press **Enter**.

Notes:

• For example, you could have a folder named Fun Sites, another for News Sites, and yet another for sites relating to Project X.

• You can add subfolders within folders. In the illustration in this procedure, you could create a new subfolder within the News folder.

Organize Favorites in Folders

Create new folders and place shortcuts in them to organize your favorites.

1   Click **Go To, Favorite Places**. The Favorite Places list opens.

Notes:

- You can also work with favorite places by opening the Personal Filing Cabinet. See **Personal Filing Cabinet**.

2 Click the folder to contain the new folder.

NOTE: For example, to place the new folder in the Favorite Places folder, click that folder.

3 Click Add Folder .

4 Type the name of the new folder and press **Enter**.

5 Drag the icon for a favorite place over to the new folder to store it in new folder.

Notes:

- The **Go To** menu lists a number of sites that you can go to by opening the menu and clicking the site or by pressing the shortcut key displayed next to the site name. You can replace any of these with your own favorite sites.

Create Shortcuts on the Go To Menu

1 Click **Go To**, **Edit Go To Menu**. The Favorite Places window opens.

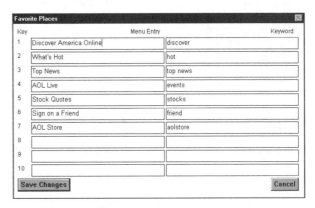

2 In the left column, type the name of the site as you want it to appear on the Go To menu.

3 In the right column, type the keyword that you use to access the site.

4 Click Save Changes .

Go to a Favorite Place

Jump to a favorite location.

1 Click **Go To**, **Favorite Places**. The Favorite Places list opens.

2 Double-click the site name.

Navigate: Go To Web Pages

Use these techniques to navigate the Web. AOL keeps track of pages that you have visited during the current session, so you can quickly return to them.

Notes:

• Stop loading a page (usually because it is taking too long to load).

Cancel a Jump

• Press **Esc**.

• Click .

Notes:

• Hyperlinks are "hot" text and graphics on a page. When you click a hyperlink, it takes you to another page. Hyperlink text is usually blue and underlined. Graphics can also be hyper-links.

Go to a Site by Selecting a Hyperlink

Click hyperlink to jump to the page.

> NOTE: When you move the mouse pointer over a hyperlink, the pointer looks like:

Notes:

• Use this procedure when you know the site address.

• Type an HTTP address (example: *http://www.aol.com*), a Gopher address (example: *gopher:// gopher.nd.edu*), or FTP address (example: *FTP.//ftp.bobs.house. org*).

• You can copy an address (**Ctrl+C**) from an e-mail message or other document and then paste it (**Ctrl+V**) into the Keyword window.

Go to a Site By Entering an Address

1 Press **Ctrl+K** to open the Keyword window.

2 Type the address and press **Enter**.

> NOTE: If the Web browser window is open, you can type the address in the address box under the Web browser toolbar.

Notes:

- AOL keeps track of Internet sites that you have visited during the current session in the history list. A session begins when you connect to the Internet and ends when you exit the browser. You can go directly to a page by selecting it from the history list.

- Or, move between the pages that you last displayed by clicking the Back and Forward buttons in the Browser toolbar. For example, return to the last page that you visited and then return to the current page.

Go to Recently Visited Page

- Click the drop-down arrow in the address box on the toolbar in the Web browser to open the list of pages you have visited. Click the page to go to.

OR

- Click ⬅ Back or ➡ Forward to go to the previous/next page.

Go to the Search Page

Go to NetFind, the AOL search page on the Web. Find newsgroups, people, businesses, and Web sites. To use a different search page, see **Navigate: Search Page**.

Click 🔍 Search on the browser toolbar.

Notes:

- The default home page is the America Online page (*http://www.aol.com*). To change it, see **Navigate: Home Page**.

Go to the Home Page

Click 🏠 Home on the browser toolbar.

Notes:

- To add a site to favorite places, see **Navigate: Favorite Places**.

Go to a Favorite Page

1   Click **Go To**, **Favorite Places**. The Favorite Places list opens.

2   Double-click the name of the site to go to.

73

Navigate: Home Page

Whenever you connect to the Internet, your home page is the first page to display. By default, the America Online page is your home page. Use this procedure to choose a new home page.

Mem**b**ers ➡ Preferences

Notes:

• The home page is the page that displays when you connect to the Web by clicking the World Wide Web button on the AOL toolbar or by pressing **Ctrl+K** and typing WWW. You can also go to the home page by clicking the Home button on the Web browser toolbar.

• You can change the home page whether you are working online or offline.

• The home page is also called the start page.

Change the Home Page

The default home page is the America Online home page (*http://www.aol.com*). Use this procedure to display a different home page such as one of your favorite search pages.

1   Click **Members**, **Preferences**, then click the .

    OR

    Click ⌗ **Prefs** on the browser toolbar if the Web browser is active.

2   Click the **Navigation** tab.

3   Select **Start Page** from the **Page** list if it is not already displayed. (Click the ▼ drop-down arrow to open the list.)

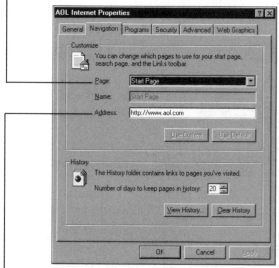

NOTE: *Depending on your system configuration, the WWW Preferences dialog box might display instead of the AOL Internet Properties dialog box. Use the Home Page text box to type the address of the home page.*

4   *Type the address of the new home page.*

OR

Click Use Current if the page is currently displayed.

5   Click OK .

Notes:

• Resets the start page to the AOL home page.

Reset the Default to the AOL Home Page

1   Click **Members**, **Preferences**, then click www .

OR

Click Prefs on the browser toolbar if the Web browser is active.

2   Click the **Navigation** tab in the AOL Internet Properties dialog box.

3   Click Use Default .

4   Click OK .

Notes:

• Go to the home page any time the Web browser is active.

Go To the Home Page

Click Home .

Navigate: Internet Search Page

America Online provides the NetFind search page for locating information on the Internet in Gopher sites, Web pages, and newsgroups. The AOL search page is the default search tool but you can change to a different one.

Notes:

- The AOL NetFind search page uses the Excite search engine, a popular tool for locating information on the Web. From the NetFind search page, you can browse through categories of topics or you can find information on specific topics using search phrases.

Go to the AOL Search Page

1   Click ⟨Q Search⟩ on the browser toolbar if the Web browser is active.

OR

Press **Ctrl+F**. Double-click **Find on the Internet with NetFind** in the Resources list (Places and Things tab).

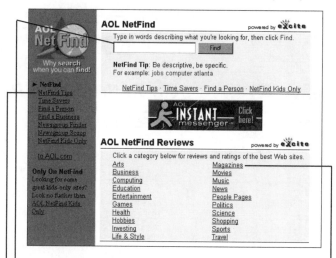

2   Some ways to locate topics on the NetFind page:

- Type a search phrase and click the **Find** button.
- Click the **NetFind Tips** hyperlink to get help on using the search page.
- Click a category in the **AOL NetFind Reviews** list to find popular sites on a variety of subjects.

Change the Search Page

AOL uses Internet Explorer as its browser. If you use a different browser, follow the instructions for your browser to change the home page.

1 Display the new search page if you want to have AOL automatically add the page address.

2 Click **Members**, **Preferences** and click ⊞ .

OR

Click ⌊☼ Prefs⌋ on the Web browser toolbar.

3 Click the **Navigation** tab.

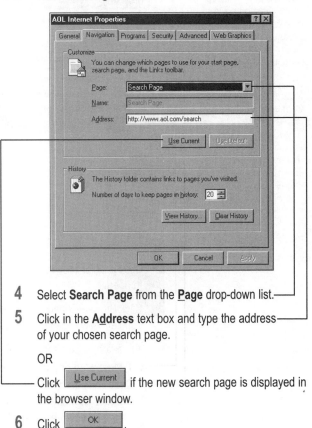

4 Select **Search Page** from the **Page** drop-down list.

5 Click in the **Address** text box and type the address of your chosen search page.

OR

Click ⌊Use Current⌋ if the new search page is displayed in the browser window.

6 Click ⌊ OK ⌋.

Navigate: Search for AOL Locations

Browse for interesting places to visit on America Online or enter a word or phrase to find all AOL locations that might have the information you are looking for.

Notes:

- One way to explore AOL is to use the Find feature. Browse through areas of AOL or enter a word or phrase to search all AOL areas for a particular topic.

- Using the Find feature is different from using Keyword (Ctrl+K). Use Keyword when you want to go to a particular location and know the keyword that will get you there. Use Find to search all areas of AOL for sites that mention a particular topic.

Find AOL Locations

1 Press **Ctrl+F** to open the AOL Find window.

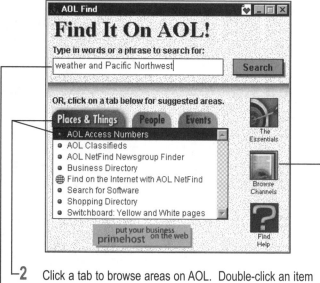

2 Click a tab to browse areas on AOL. Double-click an item to open.

3 Click Browse Channels to browse channel areas by topic. You can view locations by area or by a particular topic.

4 To search all areas for a topic:

  a. Type a word or phrase to search for. Use the following guidelines when entering a search phrase:

- Enter as many words as you would like. For example you could enter "basketball NBA." This would find information that included both terms. (This is similar to an AND operator if you are familiar with search criteria.)

- Add "not" to exclude words. For example, you could search for "basketball not NBA."

- The Find feature does not use the OR search operator. In other words, you cannot look for "basketball or NBA."

- Find does not perform a full-text search of the information in all locations. It searches an index created for the purpose of finding locations.

- Use AND, OR, and NOT to define your search when entering a search phrase to locate topics. Use NOT to exclude topics. Examples: shopping and shoes, shopping not shoes, politics and Florida

b. Click **Search** . If sites are found that might match your topic, the Search Results window opens with a list of relevant sites.

NOTE: All sites in the Search Results window are relevant to your topic. The sites that are the closest match appear at the top of the list.

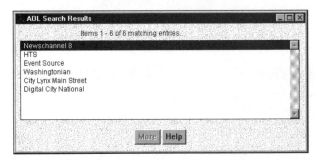

c. Double-click an entry to go to the location.

NOTE: If you are not interested in visiting a listed site, click ☒ to close the Search Results list. You can set up a different search in the AOL Find window.

Navigate: Web Browser

A Web browser is the software that you use to navigate Web pages on the Internet. When you go to a Web page, the page opens in the browser window. AOL uses a modified form of Internet Explorer as its Web Browser.

Go To → Keyword... → www

Notes:

- To connect to the Web, you must have the latest version of the AOL software. These are version 3.0 for Windows and version 2.7 for the Macintosh. To upgrade to the newest version (its free), press **Ctrl+K** and type UPGRADE.

- There are many links to Web pages throughout AOL. When you jump to a location from an AOL site, you know that you are on the Web if the site is displayed in the browser window. Whenever you go to a Web site, the Web browser is activated.

- To get AOL online help on using the Web, press **Ctrl+K** and type NET HELP in the Keyword window. Press **Enter**.

The Browser Window

Browser toolbar. See the following page for a description of the buttons on the toolbar.

Address box. Shows the address of the page displayed in the window. Click the ▼ drop-down arrow to open a list of sites you have visited during the current session. You can click a site address to return to the site.

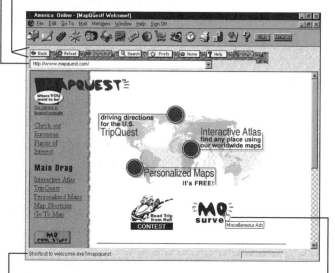

Hyperlink pointer. When you place the mouse button over a hyperlink, it changes to a hand. This particular hyperlink shows a pop-up description. A hyperlink is text or a graphic that you click to jump to a different page or to a different location on the same page.

Status bar. Shows varying status information, depending on the current action such as the progress of loading when opening a Web page. In the illustration, it shows the name of the hyperlink that the pointer is positioned on.

The Browser Toolbar

Return to the last page you viewed.

Go to the next page when browsing through previously viewed pages.

Redisplay and update the page. Use when you enable graphics and want to see the graphics on the current page. (See **Navigate: Disable Graphics on Web Pages**.) Or, if the page that you are viewing has changed since you displayed it, reload it to get the updated information.

Go to your search page. See **Navigate: Web Search Page**.

Customize your browser by setting Web preferences.

Go to your home page. By default, this is the AOL home page. To change the home page, see **Navigate: Home Page**.

Go to the AOL Help page on the Web.

Cancel loading a page. Usually you cancel when the page is taking too long to load.

Navigate: Work with Information on a Web Page

Copy text from Web pages into a document, save pages and graphics, print a page, and copy a Web page address from a hyperlink.

Notes:

- Copy text from a Web page and paste it into a document. You cannot paste into another Web page.

Copy From a Web Page to a Document

1 Drag across the text to copy.

   OR

   Press **Ctrl+A** to select all the text on the page.

2 Press **Ctrl+C** to copy the selection.

3 Switch to the document to contain the information.

   NOTE: Start up your word processor or other program if necessary and open a document in which to paste the information.

4 Press **Ctrl+V** to paste the information into the document.

Notes:

- To set margins, customize headers and footers, and other page settings, click **File**, **Print Setup**.

Print a Page

1 Display page to print.

2 Press **Ctrl+P**.

3 Select options in the Print dialog box as desired.

4 Click OK .

Notes:

- You can save a Web page in a separate file on disk in HTML format. You can open the file in a text editor or word processing program.

Save a Page in an HTML File

1 Display page to save.

2 Press **Ctrl+S**.

3 Type a **File name** and select a location for the file in the Save As dialog box.

4 Click Save .

82

Save a Graphic

1 Right-click an image on a page.

2 Click **Save Picture As**.

3 Type a **File name** and select a folder for the file in the Save As dialog box.

4 Click **Save**.

> NOTE: Depending on your system configuration, this dialog box might differ slightly. You might need to click OK rather than Save.

View the Address of a Hyperlink

1 Right-click the hyperlink.

2 Click **Properties**.

Copy the Address of a Hyperlink

1 Right-click the hyperlink.

2 Click **Copy Shortcut**.

3 Open the document to copy the address to.

4 Press **Ctrl+V**.

Newsgroups: Find a Newsgroup

Find newsgroups by searching for newsgroup names in America Online. To search for newsgroups by topic, go to the Internet.

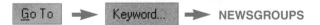

Go To ➡ Keyword... ➡ NEWSGROUPS

Notes:

- AOL's search facility is limited to searching newsgroup names. To locate newsgroups by topic, use DejaNews on the Internet. The address is *http//www.dejanews. com*. To go to this page, press **Ctrl+K**, type the address in the Keyword box, and press **Enter**. For more information, see **Newsgroups: Use DejaNews to Explore Usenet**.

- If you are looking for current FAQs (Frequently Asked Questions) for newsgroups, you will find a list of them in *news.answers*. Usually the FAQ for the group is posted in the group, but if you cannot find it there, try this group.

- To get information on using newsgroups, read the FAQ message in *aol.newsgroups.help*.

Search Newsgroup Titles

1 Press **Ctrl+K** to open the Keyword window.

2 Type **newsgroups** and press **Enter**.

3 Click [icon] in the Newsgroups window. The Search Newsgroup Titles dialog box displays.

4 Type a Search Phrase that represents one or more parts of a newsgroup name.

Use the following guidelines when entering a search phrase:
- Join words with "and" if both words must be present. Example: aol and tx
- Join words with "or" if either word is acceptable: Example: texas or tx
- Add "not" to exclude words. Example: aol and tx not politics

84

Notes:

- Use America Online's own neighborhood newsgroups to make contact with people in a specific area. National newsgroups are discussion groups by country. The discussions in these groups revolve around national politics and general trends in the country. You can find newsgroups devoted to regional politics, cities, jobs available, etc. New neighborhood newsgroups are announced in *aol.neighborhood. announce.* Search for "aol and neighborhood" in step 4 to get a complete list of these newsgroups. Once you become familiar with the names for these neighborhood newsgroups, you will easily be able to find newsgroups for a particular country or region. For example, *aol.neighborhood. nation.united-kingdom* is a national newsgroup for the United Kingdom. The newsgroup named *aol.neighborhood.wa* is a regional newsgroup for the state of Washington.

5 Click **Search** to display the results of your search.

   NOTE: If no groups matching your search phrase were found, you are returned to the Search Newsgroups window.

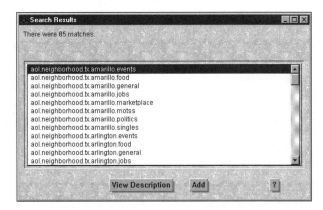

6 Double-click on a newsgroup to see a description of the group if desired.

7 Click **Add** to subscribe to the newsgroup if desired.

8 Click ⊠ to close windows when finished.

Newsgroups: Post a Group Message

Post a reply to a group message or create a new message to post. You can also respond to a group message by replying to the author of a message by e-mail.

Notes:

- You must be subscribed to a newsgroup to post messages.

- If you create a new message, the message does not become part of an existing mail thread. Your message will be the first in a new mail thread (if there are any responses).

- If you post a reply to a message, your reply is added to the list of messages in the message thread. When you create the reply, the Subject line is filled in for you. Do not change the Subject line or your mail will not be posted as part of the original mail thread.

- You can send a reply in the form of a private e-mail message. Send private e-mail when your message wouldn't be of interest to group members. For tips on newsgroup netiquette, see **Newsgroups: An Overview**.

Post a Group Message

1   Display the message to reply to or open any newsgroup message to create a new one.

   *NOTE: See **Open a Newsgroup** in **Newsgroups: Work with Newsgroups Offline** or **Newsgroups: Work with Newsgroups Online** for help opening a message.*

2   To include all or part of the original message in your reply, select the text to include.

3   Click **Reply to Group** to reply to the message. The Post Response window opens if you are online, and a similar window opens if you are offline.

   OR

   Click Send New Message if working online or click **New Message** if working offline to create an entirely new message to post to the group. The Post New Message window opens. The New Message window is similar to the Post Response window.

   NOTE: To send an e-mail message to the author of the original message, click E-mail to Author if working online and Reply to Author if working offline. This opens a mail message window with the recipient's name filled in for you.

Notes:

- Send a test message to the *aol.newsgroups. test* group to make sure that your messaging is working properly.

- You can work online or offline but you can only post messages to newsgroups that you have downloaded if you are working offline. See **Newsgroups: Work with Group Message Offline** for instructions on downloading newsgroup messages.

- If working online, you send the message immediately. If working offline, you must send it later. Your message is placed in the Outgoing Messages folder (located in the Newsgroups folder) in your Personal Filing Cabinet. Use a FlashSession to send messages that you created while working offline. See **FlashSessions**.

- In a moderated group, one or more individuals reads every message before posting to the group to make sure each message is appropriate and helpful to members. Moderated group discussions are often more focused than unmoderated discussions.

- Your message might not be posted to the group discussion immediately. Newsgroup servers receive tens of thousands of messages every day, and posting is not always immediate.

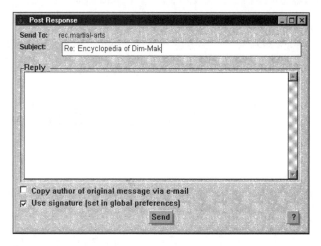

4   Type your message in the Reply text box.

5   If working online, fill out the following options (not available if working offline):

- Click the **Copy author of original message via e-mail** option to send a copy of the posting to the author of the original message through e-mail if desired. (This option is available only if you are replying to a message rather than creating a new one.)

- Mark or unmark **Use signature** as desired to include or not include your signature.

   NOTE: *You must have added your signature in Newsgroup preferences. See **Newsgroups: Set Newsgroup Preferences and Controls**.*

6   Click **Send** if working online.

OR

Click **Send Later** if working offline.

NOTE: *Activate a FlashSession to send messages when working offline. See **FlashSessions**.*

Newsgroups: Remove a Newsgroup

Keeping up with newsgroup messages can keep you busy. When a newsgroup no longer interests you, remove it from your list of subscribed newsgroups.

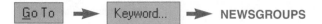

Go To ➡ Keyword... ➡ **NEWSGROUPS**

Notes:

- To remove yourself from a group, first go to the list of your personal newsgroups (the newsgroups to which you are subscribed).

Unsubscribe to a Group

1 Press **Ctrl+K** to open the Keyword window.

2 Type **newsgroups** and press **Enter**. The Newsgroups window displays.

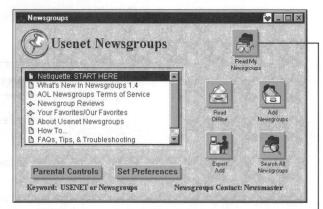

3 Click **Read My Newsgroups** to open the list of newsgroups of which you are a member.

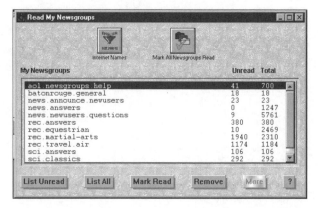

- If you ever want to join again, you can subscribe at any time. To join a group, see **Newsgroups: Subscribe to a Group**.

4 Click the group to remove.

5 Click **Remove**.

6 Click **OK** at the prompt notifying you that you have been removed from the group.

   NOTE: The group remains in the Read My Newsgroups window. The next time you open the window, the group will be gone.

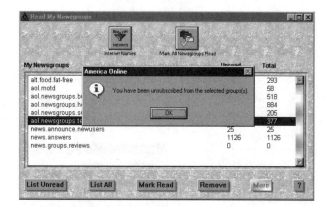

7 Repeat from step 4 as desired to remove yourself from more groups.

8 Click ⊠ to close the window.

Newsgroups: Set Newsgroup Preferences and Controls

Set up your signature so that you can add it to the end of group messages that you post. Set parental controls to determine which newsgroups your children can access or to block all newsgroups for a screen name.

Go To ➡ Keyword... ➡ NEWSGROUPS

Notes:

- You must be online to set newsgroup preferences.

- Probably the most widely used newsgroup preference is the signature. Many newsgroup members use the signature to identify themselves in discussions. Some members add a favorite (short) quotation or a nickname. You can enter anything, such as a company name, address, e-mail name, or whatever you choose.

- If you add a signature, keep it short. Newsgroup members do not want to repeatedly download messages with long signatures.

- By default, messages are ordered by date, with the most recent mess-ages last. This means that when you read a message thread, the original message is at the top of the thread followed by replies to the original.

Set Newsgroup Preferences

1   Press **Ctrl+K** to open the Keyword window.

2   Type **newsgroups** and press **Enter**.

3   Click **Set Preferences** in the Newsgroups window. The Preferences window opens.

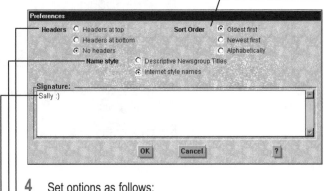

4   Set options as follows:

- **Headers**. Automatically add information about the article in either the top (**Headers at top**) or bottom (**Headers at bottom**) of newsgroup messages. Header information includes name of the person posting the article, e-mail address, and other information.

- **Sort order**. Set the order in which messages are listed, by date or alphabetically by subject line.

  NOTE: *Add headers to include information about the message at the top or the bottom of the window. Return to preferences to disable this option if the information becomes too cumbersome.*

- **Name style**. Display newsgroups by their names or by description (**Descriptive Newsgroup Titles**).

- **Signature**. Your signoff signature. You can add this signature at the end of messages that you post. Signatures should be no longer than 3 lines. The shorter the better.

5   Click **OK**.

Set Newsgroup Parental Controls

1   Press **Ctrl+K** to open the Keyword window.

2   Type **newsgroups** and press **Enter** to open the Newsgroups window.

3   Click **Parental Controls**.

4   Click the screen name to change and click **Edit** in the Parental Controls window. The Blocking Criteria window opens.

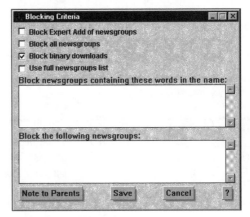

5   Set blocking options as follows:

- **Block Expert Add of Newsgroups**. Prevents the user from bypassing parental controls by subscribing to a newsgroup using the Expert Add method.

- **Block all newsgroups**. The user cannot open any newsgroup. A message appears whenever he or she tries to open a group in windows that lists newsgroups.

- **Block binary downloads**. Prevents the user from downloading from newsgroups.

- **Use full newsgroups list**. If you leave this option cleared, newsgroups with sexually explicit names will not be included in the search results. In addition, newsgroups that AOL has not yet reviewed for these names are not included in the search results. If you check the option, the user can search all newsgroups without these restrictions.

- Use the remaining text boxes to enter specific newsgroup names, or words that appear in newsgroup names that you wish to block.

6   Click **Save**.

Newsgroups: Subscribe to a Group

To participate in a newsgroup, the first thing you do is subscribe to it. After subscribing, you can download, read, and reply to messages.

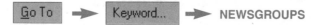

Go To ➡ Keyword... ➡ NEWSGROUPS

Notes:

- Newsgroups are located on the Internet. The newsgroup screens that you work with are the familiar America Online screens. AOL has set up an interface (news-reader) for newsgroups that makes them easy to use. There are over 20,000 newsgroups available to you through America Online.

- For a list of news-group category names, see **Newsgroups: An Overview**. In addition to the categories listed in that section, the America Online newsgroup server includes an **aol.** category of news-groups. You will find the new user news-groups in this cate-gory among others.

- Once you subscribe to a newsgroup, you can post messages in the group discus-sion as described in **Newsgroups: Post a Group Message**. You do not, however, have to participate in a discussion. You can just subscribe to a group and read messages.

Subscribe to a Newsgroup

1 Press **Ctrl+K** to open the Keyword window.

2 Type **newsgroups** and press **Enter**.

3 Click [icon] in the Newsgroups window.

   NOTE: There might be a pause while AOL gets news-groups. There are over 20,000 newsgroups in the list that it is loading.

4 Click a newsgroup category, then click **List Topics**. The Topics window displays.

   The Topics window lists topics of discussion in the news-group category. Each topic is a subcategory of the news-group category that you selected in step 4.

   The Newsgroups list shows the number of individual newsgroups in each topic.

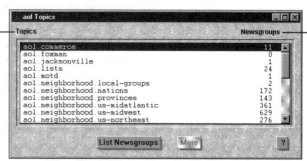

5 Click a topic and click **List Newsgroups**. The Newsgroups window opens.

• Before you subscribe
to a newsgroup,
browse through
messages posted in
the group. You can
browse newsgroup
message titles to see
topics that have
come under discus-
sion recently. Read
some of the
messages posted in
the group. This will
give you a feel for
what the group is
about, the level of
discussion, the kinds
of topics they
discuss, and the way
members relate to
the discussion.

• AOL automatically
subscribes you to
new user news-
groups. Read the
articles in these
groups to learn
Usenet netiquette,
how to find FAQs
(frequently asked
questions) for each
newsgroup, and
other important infor-
mation. For example,
*news.announce.
newusers* and
news.answers are
areas where impor-
tant messages are
posted. To get
comprehensive infor-
mation on using
newsgroups in AOL,
read the FAQ
message in
aol.newsgroups.help.

• If a group no longer
interests you, unsub-
scribe to remove your-
self from the group.
See **Newsgroups:
Remove a
Newsgroup**.

6 To find out more about listed newsgroups or to subscribe
to a group:

• The Newsgroups lists shows the available newsgroups.

• The number of subjects currently posted in the group is
displayed. A subject is the title of a message posted in
the group as part of the group discussion. To browse
subjects, click the **List Subjects** button. To browse
entire messages, click the **Read Messages** button.

• To see a description of the newsgroups listed in the
Newsgroups window, click the **Internet Names** button.
(Most, but not all newsgroups are included.)

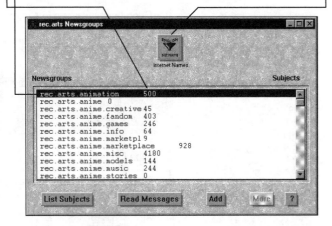

• To subscribe to a newsgroup, click the newsgroup name
and click **Add**.

7 Click **☒** to close windows when finished.

Newsgroups: Work with Group Messages

Print a message, save a message in a separate file, and find a message by searching the message Subject text.

Notes:

- Locate messages by searching through the subject of all messages in a newsgroup. You can only search a single newsgroup at a time.

- This function is available only for AOL members using Microsoft Windows.

- Only messages that are marked as Unread are searched. If you have read a message, it is not included in the search.

- To use this procedure you need to open the newsgroup that you want to search. See **Open a Newsgroup** in either **Newsgroups: Work with Newsgroups Offline** or **Newsgroups: Work with Newsgroups Online** depending on whether you are working online or offline.

Search Message Subjects

1 Open the newsgroup to search.

2 Click **Edit**, **Find in Top Window**. The Search dialog box opens.

3 Type the text to find.

4 Press **Enter**. The next message with the specified text in the Subject is highlighted in the list of messages.

5 Click ![Find Next] to find the next message. Repeat as necessary.

6 Click ![X] to close the Search dialog box when finished.

Print a Message

1 Open the message to print.

2 Click **File**, **Print Setup** to set options such as the page orientation, printer settings, and paper settings if desired. When finished, Click [OK].

3 Press **Ctrl+P**. The Print dialog box displays.

4 Set options as desired.

5 Click [OK].

Save a Message

1 Open the message to save.

2 Press **Ctrl+S**. The Save File As dialog box opens.

3 Display a different folder to store message in, if desired.
   NOTE: The default folder is the Download folder in the AOL directory.

4 Type a file name.

5 Click [Save].
   NOTE: Depending on your system configuration, the box might have an OK button rather than a Save button.

Newsgroups: Work with Group Messages Offline

Download unread newsgroup messages to work with them offline. Once downloaded, you can work with messages without being connected to AOL.

Go To ➡ Keyword... ➡ NEWSGROUPS

Notes:

- Downloading messages copies them to your hard disk, where they are placed in the Newsgroups folder in the Personal Filing Cabinet. A separate folder is created for each downloaded newsgroup.

- You can download one or more individual newsgroups or all newsgroups to which you subscribe.

- For a quick and easy way to download messages, see **FlashSessions**.

- It can take a while to download messages. During the download process, you cannot work in AOL.

Download Newsgroup Messages

1 Press **Ctrl+K** to open the Keyword window.

2 Type **newsgroups** and press **Enter**. The Newsgroups window displays.

3 Click [icon] to open the Choose Newsgroups window.

4 To specify newsgroups to download:
- Click a newsgroup in the **Subscribed Newsgroups** list and click **Add**. Repeat to add individual newsgroups to the list of **Newsgroups to read offline**.
- Click **Add All** to add all newsgroups to the list of **Newsgroups to read offline**.

  NOTE: AOL retains these settings. That way, you can periodically run a FlashSession to download new messages from the groups listed in the Choose Newsgroups window.

5 Click **OK**.

6 Click **Mail**, **Set Up FlashSession**. The FlashSessions window displays.

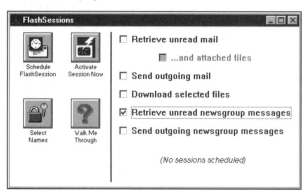

96

- Only unread messages are downloaded. When you open a newsgroup message while working online, the message is automatically marked as read. You can however, mark it as unread if you still want to download it. You can also mark individual messages, message threads, entire newsgroups, and all newsgroups as read. For example, if you don't download messages for a week, you might want to mark an entire newsgroup as read so that you are not inundated with messages. You must be working online to do this. By marking messages as read/ unread you determine which messages are downloaded.

Notes:

- Messages downloaded from newsgroups are stored in your Personal Filing Cabinet in a folder called Newsgroups. Each newsgroup is stored in a separate subfolder in the Newsgroups folder.

- To open a folder in the Personal Filing Cabinet, double-click on it.

- You can delete a message or entire folder by selecting the item and pressing **Delete**. If you delete a folder, all messages in the folder are deleted.

7   Click **Retrieve unread newsgroup messages** to mark the check box.

   *NOTE: If you also want to download mail when you download newsgroups, select **Retrieve unread mail** check box.*

8   Click **Activate Session Now**.

9   Click the **Sign off when finished** option in the Activate FlashSession Now window if you want AOL to log off after downloading.

10 Click **Begin**. AOL downloads unread messages from specified groups. A FlashSession progress indicator keeps you informed of the status of the downloading process.

Open a Newsgroup

When you open a message, it is marked as read in the Personal Filing Cabinet. Read messages are marked with a checkmark in the message list.

1   Click **File**, **Personal Filing Cabinet**.

2   View messages in the Personal File Cabinet:

   ── The Newsgroups folder stores downloaded messages.

   ── Messages are stored in a subfolder with the name of the newsgroup.

   ── Message threads (an original message and all replies to it) are stored in subfolders. Open the subfolder to view messages in the thread.

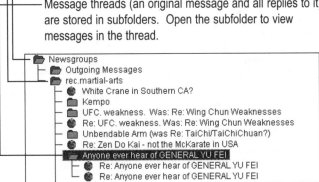

3   Double-click a message to open it.

Newsgroups: Work with Group Messages Online

Open a newsgroup of which you are a member to read messages while remaining connected to AOL.

 Go To ➡ Keyword... ➡ NEWSGROUPS

Notes:

- Because reading messages online contributes to network traffic, you should download messages and read them offline if you are going to be spending a lot of time in newsgroups. See **Newsgroups: Work with Messages Offline**.

- When you open a message, it is automatically marked as read. You can also manually mark messages as read. You might do this, for example, if you will be downloading unread messages to work with them offline and you want to exclude certain messages from being included in the download. Messages marked as read will not be downloaded. Or, you can mark messages that you have read as unread so that they will be included.

Open a Newsgroup

1 Press **Ctrl+K** to open the Keyword window.

2 Type **newsgroups** and press **Enter**. The Newsgroups window displays.

3 Click ▨ to open the list of newsgroups of which you are a member.

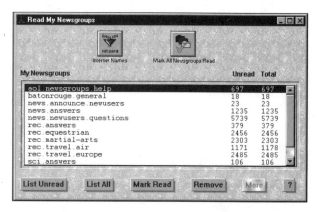

4 Use the buttons in the Read My Newsgroups window to read messages:

- Click **Mark Read** to mark all of the messages in the group as read. That way, next time you retrieve messages only new messages are displayed.

  NOTE: *You can also mark individual messages as read as described below in step 6.*

- Click **List Unread** to display unread messages only when you open the newsgroup to read messages. Messages marked as read do not appear. AOL marks messages as read when you open them. You can also mark messages as read even if you don't open the message.

98

- Newsgroup messages have a relatively short life. Tens of thousands of messages are posted to newsgroup servers every day. Old messages must be deleted to make room for new messages.

- Newsgroup messages are also known as articles.

- Click **List All** to display all message headers, even those marked as read.

5 To open a newsgroup and display messages, double-click the group name. The subject and number of messages in mail threads are listed in the Usenet Newsgroup window.

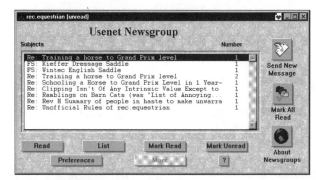

6 To work with messages:

- To open a message, double-click it. For information on working with open messages, see **Newsgroups: Work with Messages**.

- Click **Mark Read** or (on the right side of the window) to mark either the selected message or all messages as read.

- Click **Mark Unread** to mark the selected message as unread if you have opened the message but do not wish it to be marked as read.

- Click **List** to show information about the selected message.

- To display only recent messages, click **Preferences**. Type the number of days in the **Show messages no more than x days old** option. Click **Save**.

Personal Filing Cabinet

The Personal Filing Cabinet is a storage area on your hard disk. Here you will find saved and downloaded e-mail messages, downloaded files, and downloaded newsgroup messages. This is also the center for storing items to be sent in the next FlashSession and Download Manager session.

Notes:

- To automatically save copies of e-mail messages that you send and/or receive, see **E-Mail: Mail Preferences**. Saved e-mail messages are stored in the Mail/Archives/Mail You've Sent and Mail You've Read folders in the Personal Filing Cabinet.

- Mail that you retrieved using a FlashSession is located in the Mail/Incoming FlashMail folder. Mail waiting to be sent in the next FlashSession is located in the Mail/Outgoing FlashMail folder. See **FlashSessions** to send and retrieve mail in this way.

Work with Items in the Personal Filing Cabinet

1   Click **File**, **Personal Filing Cabinet** to display the Personal Filing Cabinet.

2   Work with items in the Personal Filing Cabinet as follows:
- To select an item such as a folder, file, or shortcut, click on it.
- To create a subfolder, click the folder that will contain the new subfolder. Click **Add Folder**.
- To move an item from one folder to another, drag the item between folders.
- To rename an item, right-click it and select **Rename**. You can only rename some types of items. For example, you cannot rename a standard folder such as the Mail or Newsgroups folder.
- To delete an item, right-click the item and click **Delete**. *NOTE: Deleting a folder deletes all items in the folder.*
- To display the contents of a folder in a new window, right-click the folder and click **New Window**.

3   Click ☒ when finished to close the Personal Filing Cabinet.

Notes:

- Go to the Personal Filing Cabinet to delete mail messages that you do not want to save and to organize messages that you will keep in folders. For example, you could create a folder to store all messages relating to a particular client or project. Mail will rapidly multiply, so you will want to organize mail and delete old messages. Otherwise, important messages will be difficult to locate.

- Information about files already downloaded and files waiting to be downloaded using Download Manager or a FlashSession is stored in the Download Manager folder.

- The Personal Filing Cabinet stores short-cuts to sites in the Favorite Places folder. You can orga-nize shortcuts in fold-ers, delete them, and modify them. Changes you make to favorite places in the Personal Filing Cabinet will appear on the Favorite Places button and menu item.

- Since the Personal Filing Cabinet is located on your local disk, you can work with it while you are offline or online.

Search for Text

Search all folders or folders that are currently open in the Personal Filing Cabinet.

You can search the titles of items in folders (such as the Subject text in e-mail message headers) or you can search all text (including message bodies).

1 Open the Personal Filing Cabinet. (See procedure on previous page for instructions.)

2 If searching open folders, open the folders to search.

3 Click [Search] to open the Search dialog box.

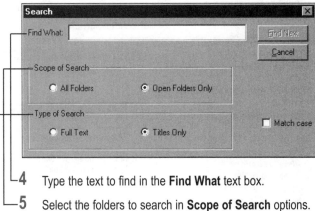

4 Type the text to find in the **Find What** text box.

5 Select the folders to search in **Scope of Search** options.

6 Select whether to search all text or titles only in **Type of Search** options.

7 Select **Match case** to find only instances of the text matching upper/lowercase as typed in the **Find What** text box if desired.

8 Click [Find Next].

Screen Names

Add up to five different screen names to use to sign on to AOL. Screen names are often used in families where each member has their own name.

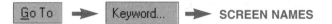

Go To ➡ Keyword... ➡ **SCREEN NAMES**

Notes:

- A screen name is the name that you use to sign on to AOL. The screen name that you use to sign on for a session is the name that appears in chat rooms, e-mail that you create, instant messages that you send, and any other place where your name is visible.

- Your screen name is also your e-mail name. It is automatically added to e-mail messages that you create, identifying you as the sender. Other AOL users send mail to your screen name.

- Create up to five screen names so that different members of your household or office can sign on to AOL with their own name. When you create a new screen name, you can set parental controls for the name. These determine which sites can be accessed whenever someone signs on using that name.

Add a Screen Name

1 Press **Ctrl+K** to open the Keyword window.

2 Type **screen names** and click ▐ **Go** ▌. The Create or Delete Screen Names dialog box displays.

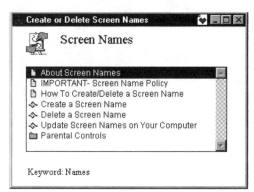

3 Double-click **Create a Screen Name** to display the Create an Alternate Screen Name dialog box.

4 Type a new screen name of 3 to 10 characters in length.

5 Click ▐ **Create a Screen Name** ▌.

   NOTE: If a name is in use but is available by attaching a number on the end of it, AOL suggests the numbered name. Type a different name or accept the suggested name.

6 Type a password for the new name twice in the Set Password dialog box.

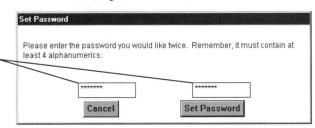

7 Click **Set Password**. The Parental Controls dialog box displays.

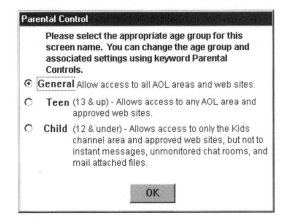

8 Click the appropriate access rights for the new name.

9 Click OK.

MS Internet Explorer

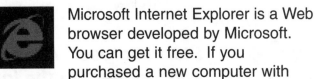 Microsoft Internet Explorer is a Web browser developed by Microsoft. You can get it free. If you purchased a new computer with Windows 95 loaded, Internet Explorer was included. To upgrade to the latest version or to obtain the program if you have access to the Web, connect to www.microsoft.com/ie and download it. If you do not already have Internet Explorer and your online service provider is America Online, CompuServe, or The Microsoft Network, connect to the above site and download the software. Internet Explorer is also available in retail stores in the Microsoft Plus! package for Windows. You can buy the package, install Internet Explorer so that you can connect to the Web and then download the latest version.

Start Microsoft Internet Explorer

Start Microsoft Internet Explorer and connect to the Internet or start it and work offline. You might want to work offline, for example, in order to set Microsoft Internet Explorer options or to view pages in the History folder.

The Internet

Notes:

- When you set up Microsoft Internet Explorer, the setup program should place an Internet icon on your desktop. If you cannot find the icon, use the Windows Start menu to start Internet Explorer.

- By default, the start page that first appears each time you connect using Microsoft Internet Explorer, is the Microsoft home page. You can change the start page if you wish. See the section called **Start Page**.

Start Microsoft Internet Explorer and Connect to the Internet

1 Double-click The Internet located on the desktop.

OR

Click **Start** on the Windows Taskbar to open the Start menu (**Ctrl+Esc** also opens the Start menu) and click **Programs**, **Internet Explorer**.

2 If a dialog box appears, enter information such as your password, if necessary, and click Connect . The information in this dialog box varies depending on your service provider. For example, the Connect To dialog box in the illustration appears if CompuServe is your service provider.

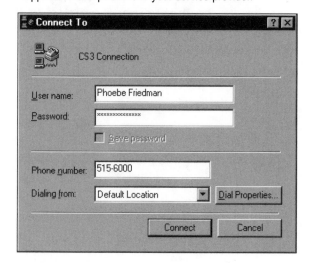

106

A message box displays informing you of the status of your connection to the network.

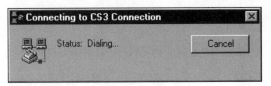

When successfully connected, your start page displays.

Start Microsoft Internet Explorer and Work Offline

1 Double-click The Internet located on the desktop.

OR

Click **Start** on the Windows Taskbar to open the Start menu (**Ctrl+Esc** also opens the Start menu) and click **Programs**, **Internet Explorer**.

2 At the dialog box, click or press **Esc**.

The Microsoft Internet Explorer window appears.

3 Set options as desired.

4 Press **Alt+F4** to exit.

Customize the Microsoft Internet Explorer Toolbar

The Microsoft Internet Explorer toolbar is at the top of the window. Use the tools on this toolbar to quickly issue commands. Use the following procedures to change the appearance of the toolbar.

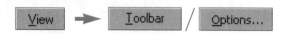

View ➡ Toolbar / Options...

Notes:

• Hide the toolbar when you want to use the entire window to view a Web page. Repeat the procedure to redisplay it.

Notes:

• By default, Microsoft Internet Explorer displays all toolbar elements.

Show/Hide the Toolbar

Click **View**, **Toolbar**.

Customize the Toolbar

Set the elements of the toolbar that are displayed by default whenever you start Microsoft Internet Explorer. For example, you can show or hide the toolbar and/or the address bar and text labels on tools.

1 Click **View**, **Options**.

2 Click the **General** tab in the Options dialog box.

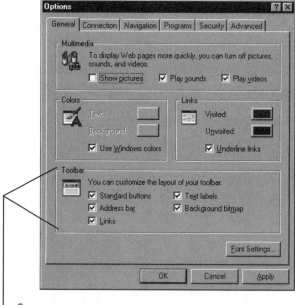

3 Set **Toolbar** options as follows:

• Click **Standard buttons** to show or hide the toolbar by default. If you deselect the option, the toolbar is not displayed when you start Microsoft Internet Explorer. To display the toolbar, click **View**, **Toolbar**.

*NOTE: When you hide the toolbar using this setting, the Address bar remains displayed. To also hide the Address bar, clear the **Address bar** option as described below.*

• Click **Address bar** to show or hide the Address bar. The Address bar is part of the toolbar and shows the address of the currently displayed page and lists previously displayed pages or files.

• Click **Links** to show or hide the Links button on the toolbar.

• Click **Text labels** to show or hide text labels on the toolbar. If you clear the option, toolbar buttons show only a graphic.

• Click **Background bitmap** to show or hide the background texture of the toolbar.

4 Click [Apply] if desired to see how the Microsoft Internet Explorer window will look with the current toolbar options.

5 Click [OK].

Customize the Microsoft Internet Explorer Window

Customize Microsoft Internet Explorer window display by changing the font size on a Web page, setting the window colors.

 View → Options...

Notes:

- By default, Microsoft Internet Explorer uses the Windows color scheme. Use this procedure to use different colors.

- If you change the color scheme, you can use this procedure to reset colors back to the Windows default at any time.

Set Window Colors

1 Click **View**, **Options**.

2 Click the **General** tab in the Options dialog box.

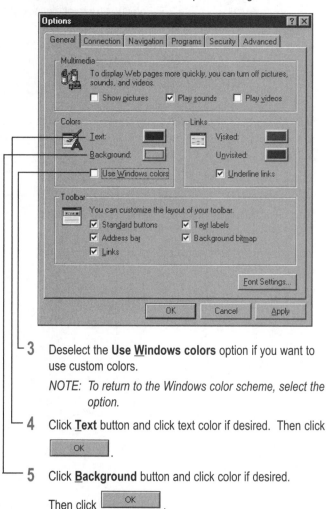

3 Deselect the **Use Windows colors** option if you want to use custom colors.

   NOTE: To return to the Windows color scheme, select the option.

4 Click **Text** button and click text color if desired. Then click
   `OK`.

5 Click **Background** button and click color if desired.
   Then click `OK`.

6 Click `OK`.

- Make text easier to read by increasing the font size or fit more on a page by decreasing the font size. This does not work for all Web pages.

- You might want to set the font to a smaller size before you print so that you use less paper and then switch back to a larger font for viewing pages.

Change the Font Size

- Click  to set text to the next larger font size.

NOTE: The Font toolbar button cycles through available font size settings. Each time you click the button, Microsoft Internet Explorer displays text on the page in the next smaller or larger font size. You can go directly to a specific font size setting if you use the menu command.

OR

- Click **View**, **Fonts** and select a size.

111

Favorite Pages: Creating Shortcuts

Create shortcuts to sites that you visit often so that you can go to them quickly. Store your shortcuts in the Favorites folder or place them directly on the desktop.

 or

Notes:

- After you add the page to Favorites, you can easily jump to the page by using the **Go to a Favorite Page** procedure on the following page.

- If you have too many shortcuts in your Favorites folder, create subfolders in the Favorites folder. For example, you might start adding shortcuts in a subfolder called "Fun Sites" or "Search Pages" or "Project X."

Add the Current Page to Favorites

1 Display the site to add.

2 Click **Favorites** or click .

3 Click **Add To Favorites**.

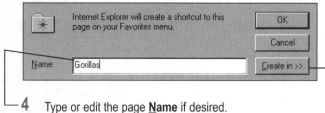

4 Type or edit the page **Name** if desired.

5 To store the shortcut in a subfolder if desired:

a. Click Create in >> . The Add to Favorites dialog box displays.

Notes:

- Favorite pages, including those in subfolders in the Favorites folder, are listed under both the Favorites menu and the Favorites button.

- Shortcuts to pages are often referred to as *bookmarks* in Internet terminology.

- For information on moving shortcuts between folders, deleting shortcuts, and other functions, see **Favorite Places: Organizing**.

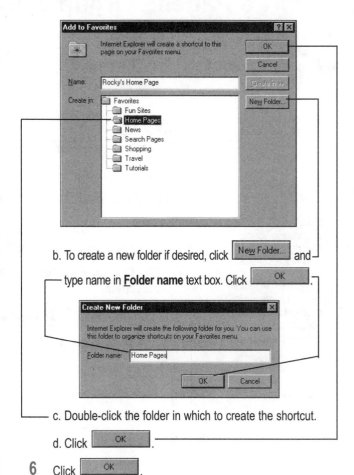

b. To create a new folder if desired, click New Folder... and type name in **Folder name** text box. Click OK.

c. Double-click the folder in which to create the shortcut.

d. Click OK.

6 Click OK.

Notes:

- Once you have added a page to the list of favorites, you can quickly jump to it by opening your list of favorites.

Notes:

- When you create a shortcut to a Web page and place it on the desktop, you can use the shortcut to start Microsoft Internet Explorer and view the page offline.

- If you can see both the desktop and the Microsoft Internet Explorer window, you can also drag the hyperlink from the window to the desktop to create a shortcut.

Go to a Favorite Page

1 Click Favorites or click **F̲avorites**.

2 If necessary, click the folder containing the shortcut.

3 Click the page to jump to.

Create a Shortcut on the Desktop

1 Display page to create shortcut to.

NOTE: If working offline, display page address in the address bar.

2 Click **F̲ile, Cr̲eate Shortcut**.

3 Click OK at the prompt.

Favorite Pages: Organizing

When you have created many shortcuts to sites, you may find it difficult to quickly locate a shortcut. Use these procedures to create new folders to store shortcuts and to move, copy, and otherwise organize shortcuts in folders.

Favorites   or   Favorites

Create a Folder to Store Shortcuts

1 Click **Favorites** or click Favorites .

2 Click **Organize Favorites**. The Organize Favorites dialog box appears.

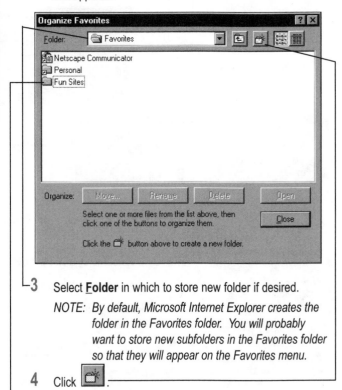

3 Select **Folder** in which to store new folder if desired.

NOTE: *By default, Microsoft Internet Explorer creates the folder in the Favorites folder. You will probably want to store new subfolders in the Favorites folder so that they will appear on the Favorites menu.*

4 Click .

5 Type new folder name and press **Enter**.

6 Repeat from step 2 as necessary to create more folders.

7 Click Close when finished.

Notes:

- Organize shortcuts that you have already created in different folders so that you can quickly find them.

Move Shortcuts Between Folders

1 Click **Favorites** or click **Favorites**.

2 Click **Organize Favorites**.

3 Drag desired shortcut to new folder.

OR

Click shortcut to move then click **Move...**. Double-click

folder to move to and click **OK**.

4 Repeat step 3 as desired to move shortcuts.

5 Click **Close** when finished.

Notes:

- An important part of organizing your shortcuts is removing those sites that you no longer visit so that you can quickly locate shortcuts that you do use.

- Use descriptive names that make it easy for you to identify shortcuts.

Rename or Delete a Shortcut

1 Click **Favorites** or click **Favorites**.

2 Click **Organize Favorites**.

3 Click shortcut to select it.

4 To rename selected shortcut if desired:

a. Click **Rename**.

b. Type new name.

c. Press **Enter**.

5 To delete selected shortcut if desired:

a. Click **Delete**.

b. Click **Yes** at the Confirm Deletion prompt.

6 Click **Close** when finished.

History List

Microsoft Internet Explorer keeps a log of the pages that you have visited during your sessions on the Internet. It stores this information in the history list. Use this information to locate addresses and visit previously viewed sites.

Go to a Site in the History List

- Click [Back] or click **Go**, **Back** to go to the last page you displayed. Repeat as desired to move back through previously viewed pages.

- Click [Forward] or click **Go**, **Forward** to move forward to the next page in the history list.

- Click **Go**, and then click the name of the page to go to.

Go to a Site in the History Folder

1 Click **Go**, **Open History List**.

2 Double-click the site that you wish to go to.

   NOTE: If you are connected to the Internet, double-clicking the site jumps to the site.

- By default, the History list stores the sites that you visit for 20 days. If you are low on disk space or if you need to store the information for a longer period, change the number of days to store history. Since Microsoft Internet Explorer stores not only the site address but also a copy of each page, the contents of the History list can take up a lot of disk space.

- You can also use this procedure to clear the History list and to view the contents of the folder.

Set Number of Days to Store Addresses in History List

1 Click **View**, **Options** to display the Options dialog box.

2 Click the **Navigation** tab.

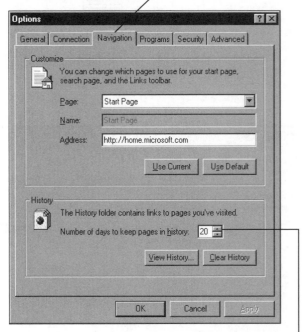

3 Type or select the **Number of days to keep pages in history**.

   NOTE: To delete all the information in the History folder if desired, click Clear History .

4 Click OK .

Navigate Pages and Sites

Move between pages while you are connected to the Internet. Go to different pages in a single site or go to another site, including sites that you have previously visited.

Notes:

- The Status bar at the bottom of the window shows you how fast the page is opening. If it takes too long to open, you can cancel the action.

Cancel a Jump

Click or press **Esc**.

Notes:

- A hyperlink is an active graphic or line of text that, when clicked, connects you to another web page, another part of the current page, or to other computers on the Internet.

- Text hyperlinks are underlined and in a different color. You can also detect hyperlinks by watching the mouse pointer. When you move the mouse pointer over a hyperlink, the pointer changes to: 🖑.

Go to a Site by Selecting a Hyperlink

Click hyperlink to open the site in the current window.

OR

Right-click hyperlink and click **Open in New Window**.

Notes:

- You can open the site in a separate window. Press **Ctrl+N** to open a new window before using this procedure.

Go to a Site By Entering an Address

1 Click the address displayed in the |Address| box.

2 Type address of site to go to.

3 Press **Enter**.

Notes:

- Move between pages that you have previously viewed. Use the toolbar buttons and Go menu to return to sites visited during the current Internet session. Or, go to sites visited in previous sessions by opening the History folder.

- For more information on history, see **History List**.

Go to Previously Visited Pages

- Click or click **Go**, **Back** to go to the last page you displayed. Repeat to move back through previously viewed pages.

- Click [Forward] or click **Go**, **Forward** to go to the next page in the history list.
- Click **Go** and click the page name on the Go menu.
- Click **Go**, **Open History Folder** and double-click the page to go to.

Notes:

- You can add pages that you frequently visit or would like to return to in the list of favorite sites on the Favorites menu. See **Favorite Pages: Creating Shortcuts**.

Go to a Favorite Page

1 Click [Favorites] or click **Favorites**.

2 Click folder to open if necessary.

3 Click name of page to go to.

Notes:

- Go to your search page at any time you are connected to the Internet.

Go to the Search Page

Click or click **Go**, **Search the Web**.

Notes:

- The Links toolbar has tools that jump to pages of interest, such as Best of the Web picks. These pages are updated often.

Show the Links Toolbar

Click [Links].

NOTE: Repeat the procedure to redisplay the Microsoft Internet Explorer toolbar.

Notes:

- The start page is the page that appears when you connect to the Internet.

Return to the Start Page

Click or click **Go**, **Start Page**.

Search Page

The search page is a Web page that you use to search for information on the Web. Use this procedure to set the default search page to your favorite search engine.

Notes:

- The default search page for Explorer is the Microsoft search page. From this page you can access the most popular search engines on the Internet, such as Yahoo, InfoSeek, Alta Vista, Lycos, Magellan and more.

- You can change the search page while you are connected to the Internet, or you can change it, before you connect, if you know the address of the new search page.

- If you have previously viewed the site you wish to use as your search page, you can copy the address from the History folder.

- To reset your search page to the default Microsoft search page, follow **Reset the Search Page**.

- For more information on search engines, see **Search Pages** at the beginning of this book.

Change the Search Page

1 Display the new search page if you want to have Internet Explorer automatically add the page address.

2 Click **View**, **Options** to display the Options dialog box.

NOTE: To copy the address from the History folder, click **Go, Open History Folder**, select the page and press **Ctrl+C**. Paste the address (**Ctrl+V**) at step 4.

3 Click the **Navigation** tab.

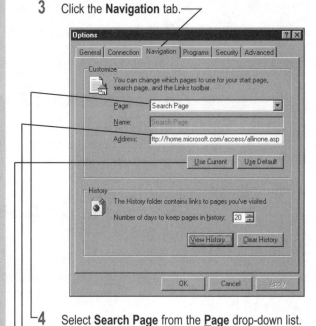

4 Select **Search Page** from the **Page** drop-down list.

5 Click in the **Address** text box and type the address of your chosen search page.

OR

Click ▭ Use Current ▭ if the new search page is currently displayed in the Internet Explorer window.

6 Click ▭ OK ▭ .

Notes:

- Resets the start page to the default Microsoft search page. Use this procedure after you have changed to a different search page.

Reset the Search Page

1 Click **View**, **Options** to display the Options dialog box.

2 Click the **Navigation** tab.

3 Click ⌈ U<u>s</u>e Default ⌉.

4 Click ⌈ OK ⌉.

Notes:

- Go to your search page at any time you are connected to the Internet.

Go to the Search Page

Click .

OR

Click **G**o, **Search** the **W**eb.

Start Page

The start page is the page that opens each time you connect to the Internet. The default start page in Internet Explorer is the Microsoft home page. This procedure tells you how to set Microsoft Explorer to open to a different start page.

Notes:

- You can change the start page while you are connected to the Internet, or you can change it before you connect if you know the address of the new start page.

- To reset the start page to the Microsoft home page, see **Reset the Start Page to the Default** procedure on the following page.

- The start page is different than the search page. The start page is the page that appears when you connect to the Web. You use the search page to find information on the Web. See the section called **Search Page**.

Change the Start Page

1 Display the new start page if you want to have Internet Explorer automatically add the page address.

2 Click **View**, **Options** to display the Options dialog box.

3 Click the **Navigation** tab.

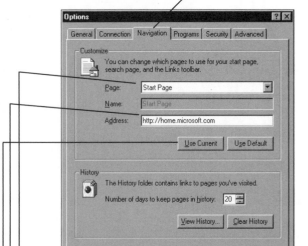

4 Select **Start Page** from the **Page** drop-down list if necessary.

5 Click in the **Address** text box and type the address of your chosen start page.

OR

Click `Use Current` if the new start page is displayed in the Internet Explorer window.

6 Click `OK`.

Notes:

- Resets the start page to the Microsoft home page. Use after you have changed the start page to a different page.

Reset the Start Page to the Default

1 Click **View**, **Options** to display the Options dialog box.

2 Click the **Navigation** tab.

3 Click .

4 Click [OK] .

Notes:

- When you are connected to the network, you can quickly return to your start page at any time using this procedure.

Go to Start Page

Click [🏠 Home] .

OR

Click **Go**, **Start Page**.

Switch to E-mail

Microsoft Internet Explorer links to your e-mail program so that you can open the program without exiting Explorer. For example, if your e-mail program is Outlook, Microsoft Internet Explorer will start Outlook when you want to send and receive messages.

Go to E-mail and Read Mail

1 or click **Go**.

2 Click **Read Mail**.

3 Retrieve and read messages using your e-mail program.

   NOTE: *Microsoft Internet Explorer remains open. You can switch back to it when finished reading mail.*

Create a Mail Message

1 Click .

2 Click **New Message**.

3 Create and send the message using your e-mail program.

   NOTE: *Microsoft Internet Explorer remains open. You can switch back to it when finished creating and sending mail.*

Create a Mail Message with a Hyperlink to a Site

1 Display Internet site for which you will create a hyperlink.

   NOTE: *If you are composing the message offline, display the address of the site in the Address text box.*

2 Click **File, Send To**.

3 Click **Mail Recipient**.

Specify Your E-mail Program

Set the e-mail program that will start when you use the e-mail function in Microsoft Internet Explorer. This might be, for example, Microsoft Outlook, Microsoft Exchange, Eudora, Pegasus, or another e-mail program. Or, your service provider might provide a mail program that you can connect to.

1 Click **View**, **Options**.

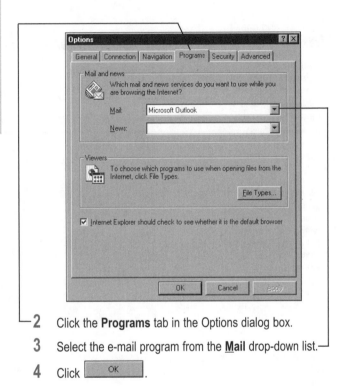

2 Click the **Programs** tab in the Options dialog box.

3 Select the e-mail program from the **Mail** drop-down list.

4 Click [OK].

View Text-Only or Text and Graphics

If you are interested in speed rather than viewing graphics on Web pages, navigating the Web is much faster if you turn off the graphic display. Use this procedure to disable or enable graphics and other multimedia.

Notes:

- You can use this procedure before or after you connect to the Internet. If you are already online, press the Refresh button after you change the graphics mode. Explorer will switch over to the new mode that you have set.

- When you view text only, Web pages load considerably faster than when you display both text and graphics. Part of the fun of exploring the Internet is the graphic elements on Web pages, but they can really slow you down.

- By default, all multimedia is enabled in Microsoft Internet Explorer.

Enable or Disable Multimedia

1 Click **View**, **Options** to display the Options dialog box.

2 Click the **General** tab.

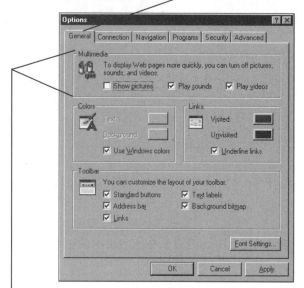

3 Select or clear **Multimedia** options as desired:

a. Click **Show pictures** to select or clear it. When cleared, Internet Explorer displays text only and does not include graphics.

b. Click **Play sounds** to enable or disable sounds.

c. Click **Play videos** to enable or disable movies.

4 Click OK.

5 Click Refresh or press **F5** to update the setting if you are connected to the Internet.

Show a Graphic in Text-Only Mode

1 Right-click the icon or placeholder on the page.

2 Click **Show Picture**. The graphic is displayed on the screen.

127

Work with Information on a Web Page

Copy information from a Web page, convert the page to an HTML document, find text on a page, and print a page.

Notes:
- Copy text from a Web page and paste it into a document. You cannot paste into another Web page.

Copy From a Web Page to a Document

1 To select information to copy, drag across text.

OR

To select the entire page, click **Edit**, **Select All**.

2 Click **Edit**, **Copy**.

3 Switch to the document to contain the information.

NOTE: Start up your word processor or other program if necessary and open a document in which to paste the information.

4 Press **Ctrl+V**.

Notes:
- Search for a word or phrase on the currently displayed page.

Search the Current Page for Information

1 Press **Ctrl+F** to display the Find dialog box.

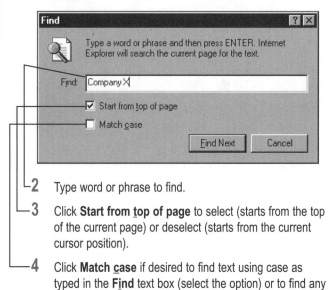

2 Type word or phrase to find.

3 Click **Start from top of page** to select (starts from the top of the current page) or deselect (starts from the current cursor position).

4 Click **Match case** if desired to find text using case as typed in the **Find** text box (select the option) or to find any text that matches, regardless of case (clear the option).

5 Click [Find Next] to locate next instance of text in document.

6 Repeat step 5 as desired.

7 Press [Cancel] to close the Find dialog box when finished.

Print a Page

1 Display page to print.

2 Press **Ctrl+P**.

3 Select desired options in the Print dialog box.

4 Click [OK] to print.

Notes:

- To set margins and other page settings, click **File**, **Page Setup**.

- To change the font size to a smaller font before printing, click **View**, **Fonts**.

Edit a Page

1 Display page to edit.

2 Click [Edit] or click **Edit**, **Current Page**.

Notes:

- Starts your word processor or other HTML editor and displays the current Web page in HTML.

Save a Page in an HTML File

1 Display page to save.

2 Click **File**, **Save As File**.

3 Type a **File name** for the file.

4 Click [Save].

Notes:

- Save the text in a Web page in a separate file on your hard drive or on a disk. Saves only the text, not graphics on a page.

Save Graphic in GIF File

1 Right-click an image on a page.

2 Click **Save Picture As**.

3 Type a **File name** for the file.

4 Click [Save].

Notes:

- GIF files are the graphics format used in Web pages.

Netscape Communicator

 Netscape Communicator is a popular browser suite that allows you to navigate the World Wide Web. In addition to its browser component, called Navigator, Netscape Communicator includes an e-mail component and a newsreader that you can use to join in newsgroup discussions.

Netscape Communicator is available for purchase at retail shops. Or, if you have access to the Internet, you can download it for a trial period of time from the Netscape home page at *http://home.netscape.com*.

Communicator: Component Bar

The Component bar is a floating palette that contains buttons for moving between the different components of Netscape Communicator.

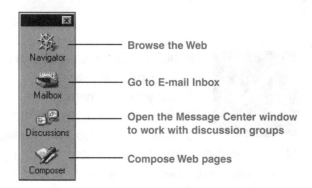

Browse the Web

Go to E-mail Inbox

Open the Message Center window to work with discussion groups

Compose Web pages

Go To a Component Using Shortcut Keys

Communicator consists of the following components:
- Navigator is a Web browser for navigating the World Wide Web.
- Use Messenger Mailbox to send and receive e-mail.
- Discussion Groups is where you go to work with newsgroup messages.
- Composer is a tool for creating your own Web pages.

Press:	To switch to:
Ctrl+1	Navigator
Ctrl+2	E-Mail
Ctrl+3	Discussion Groups (list of subscribed newsgroups)
Ctrl+Shift+2	Address Book (stores e-mail addresses)

Notes:

- You can also access Component bar commands from the Communicator menu.

Dock the Component Bar

Dock the component bar so that it becomes part of the Netscape Communicator window. The bar remains stationary in the bottom-right corner of the window on the Status bar.

Use this procedure both to dock the Component bar and to reset it to a floating palette.

- **To dock the Component bar**:

Click ⊠ in the title bar of the Component bar.

- **To return to a floating palette:**

Drag the far-left button to new position.

Notes:

- By default, the Component bar will stay on top of any open window. If the bar is in the way, use this procedure to turn off the **Always on Top** option. Then, the bar acts like any other window; the active window will be in the foreground.

Set Always on Top Option

Repeat the procedure to reset the option.

1 Right-click the title bar.

2 Click **Always on Top**.

Communicator: Go Offline

Temporarily go offline to work with information in Web pages, read and respond to messages, and perform other tasks that do not require you to be online. When finished, you can go back online.

Notes:

- Sometimes you need to perform tasks such as responding to mail messages or working with Web pages that do not require you to be online. Use this procedure to temporarily work offline without closing the connection to the Internet. You can save money if your Internet provider charges you by the hour. Some providers do not charge for offline time. When you work offline you are not contributing to network traffic, so it improves service for everyone.

- You can download e-mail messages when you go offline. For information about downloading group messages, see **Newsgroups: Work with Messages Offline**.

- You can set the startup mode to determine whether Netscape Communicator starts offline or online. See **Communicator: Startup Mode**.

1 Click **File**, **Go Offline**. The Download dialog box displays.

2 Specify the tasks to perform when you go offline:
 a. Click an option to clear it if you want to skip retrieving and/or sending messages.

 b. Click [Select Items For Download...] to select discussion group messages to download.

 *NOTE: See **Newsgroups: Work with Messages Offline** for information about downloading discussion group messages.*

3 Click [Go Offline] .

4 Work offline as desired.

Notes:

- After working offline, use this procedure to go back online to access the Internet.

- If you composed messages offline, you can send them when you go online.

Return Online

1 Click **File**, **Go Online**. The Download dialog box appears.

2 Select options in the Download dialog box for tasks to perform when you return online.

3 Click [Go Online].

135

Communicator: Start and Exit

Start Netscape Communicator and connect to the Internet. To set the startup mode (online, offline, or prompted) see **Communicator: Startup Mode**.

Netscape
Communicator

Notes:

- When you set up Netscape Communicator, the setup program places a startup icon on your desktop. If you cannot find the icon, use the Windows Start menu to start Netscape Communicator.

- This procedure assumes that the Communicator startup mode is online (Communicator connects to the Internet each time you start up). This is the default startup mode. If you have changed the startup mode to offline, click **File, Go Online** to connect to the Internet when you start Communicator. If you changed the startup mode to prompted, Communicator displays a dialog box where you can choose to connect to the Internet or work offline. To set the startup mode, see **Communicator: Startup Mode**.

Start Netscape Communicator and Connect to the Internet

1   Double-click Communicator located on the desktop.

    OR

    Click 🏁 **Start** on the Windows Taskbar to open the Start menu (**Ctrl+Esc** also opens the Start menu) and click **Programs**, **Netscape Communicator** folder, **Netscape Navigator**.

    NOTE: The first time you start Netscape Communicator, the New Profile Setup dialog box appears. Enter information about your e-mail name and service provider in the series of dialog boxes that appear. If you do not know the information, you can leave it blank for now.

2   If a dialog box appears, enter information such as your password if necessary and click [Connect]. The information in this dialog box varies depending on your service provider. For example, the Connect To dialog box in the illustration on the next page appears if CompuServe is your service provider.

    NOTE: If you work in an office with a permanent connection to the Internet through a network, you will not see a Connection dialog box. You are already connected.

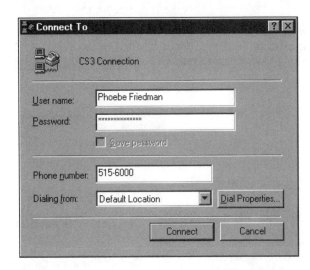

A message box displays informing you of the status of your connection to the network.

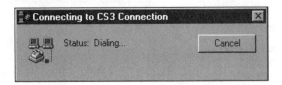

When successfully connected, your start page displays.

Exit Netscape Communicator and Disconnect

If your office is on a network with a permanent Internet connection, you do not have to disconnect.

Exactly how you disconnect depends on your service provider.

1   Click **File**, **Exit** or press **Ctrl+Q** to exit Netscape Communicator. The program closes but the connection to the network remains active.

2   Open the connection dialog box and click the **Disconnect** or other button that terminates the connection.

   NOTE: The dialog box that is available for you to disconnect from varies depending on your service provider. It might be minimized on the Windows Taskbar, in which case you first have to click the button in order to open the dialog box.

Communicator: Startup Mode

The startup mode determines whether Netscape Communicator starts in offline mode, online mode, or prompts you each time for the mode. Working in offline mode does not open the connection to the Internet.

Notes:

- Start Netscape Communicator in online mode, offline mode, or display a dialog box for you to choose whether to work online or offline each time you start Netscape Communicator.

- If you often compose e-mail and/or newsgroup messages before you go online to send them, you might want to set your startup mode to offline. Then, you can write your messages before connecting. If you sometimes write messages and other times go directly online to browse the Web, then the prompted startup mode will be the most convenient. Each time you startup, you can choose whether to work offline or connect immediately.

Set the Default Startup Mode

1   Click **Edit**, **Preferences** to display the Preferences dialog box.

2   Click **Offline** in the **Category** list to display startup options.

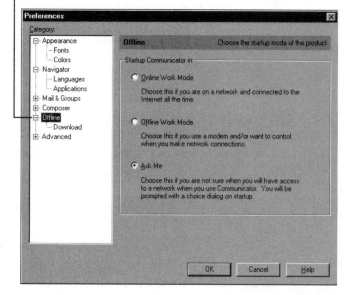

3 Click desired startup option:

- **Online Work Mode**. Connect to the Internet each time you start Netscape Communicator.

- **Offline Work Mode**. Starts Netscape Communicator without connecting to the Internet. To connect after starting in offline mode, click **File**, **Go Online**.

- **Ask Me**. Displays the Ask Me dialog box shown below each time you start Netscape Communicator:

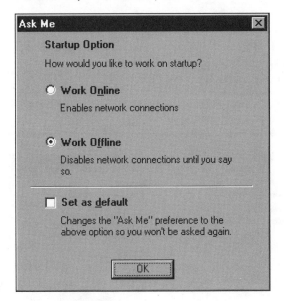

4 Click OK.

Address Book: Add Individuals to the Address Book

You can add e-mail information for individuals to the Netscape Personal Address Book so that you do not have to remember names and addresses when you send messages. Each address is stored on a separate address card.

Communicator ➡ Address Book

Notes:

- Add the information for an individual in a new address card by typing in the information. To automatically create an address book entry for the sender of a message after you open it, follow **Add Name(s) from a Message to the Address Book** procedure on the following page.

- After you add names to the address book, you can select the addresses of message recipients from the address book.

- You can also set up groups of addresses to send the same e-mail message to multiple recipients. See **Address Book: Add Mailing Lists to the Address Book**.

Add a Name to the Address Book

1 Click **Communicator**, **Address Book** to open the Address Book dialog box.

2 Click [New Card] to open the New Card dialog box.

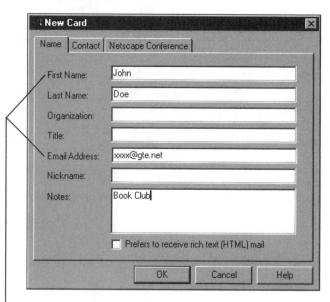

3 Fill in information in the **Name** tab.

NOTE: *The only required fields are **First Name** and **Email Address**. You must enter something in these fields.*

4 Fill in information in **Contact** tab (address and phone number information) and/or **Netscape Conference** tab (Conference server or host for Netscape Messenger conferencing) as desired.

5 Click [OK].

Add Name(s) from a Message to the Address Book

Automatically create entries in your address book from a mail message that you have received. Specify whether to add the e-mail name and address of the sender of the message only, or all names in the message, such as Cc: recipients.

1 Display message containing names to add to address book.

2 Click **Message**, **Add to Address Book**.

3 Click **Sender** to add only the sender's name.

OR

Click **All** to add the name of the sender and all other recipients of the message.

Delete an Address Card

Remove one or more entries from your address book.

1 Click **Communicator**, **Address Book** to open the Address Book dialog box.

2 Click name to select it.

3 Press **Delete**.

Address Book: Add Mailing Lists to the Address Book

You can add e-mail information to the address book so that you do not have to remember names and addresses when you send messages. Use mailing lists to send the same message to a group of individuals.

Communicator ➡ Address Book

Notes:

- A mailing list is a list of names and e-mail addresses for a group of people. When you send a message to a mailing list, the same message is sent to each individual in the list.

- Each mailing list is stored in a separate mailing list card in the address book. Each individual on the mailing list must have an address card in the address book. Before creating mailing lists, use the procedures in the **Address Book: Adding Individuals to the Address Book** section to create entries for each individual.

Add a Mailing List to the Address Book

1 Click **Communicator**, **Address Book** to open the Address Book dialog box.

2 Click [New List] to display the Mailing List dialog box.

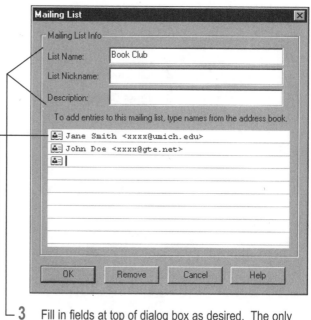

3 Fill in fields at top of dialog box as desired. The only required field is **List Name**.

4 Type a name from the address book on a line in the lower part of the dialog box. When Netscape Communicator recognizes a name, it finishes the address for you. Press **Enter**.

5 Repeat step 4 as necessary to enter recipients in the mailing list.

6 Click [OK].

Remove a Name from a Mailing List

Remove one or more individuals from a mailing list.

1 Click **Communicator**, **Address Book** to open the Address Book dialog box.

2 Double-click the list to edit in the list of addresses.

3 Click the name to remove and click [Remove].

4 Click [OK].

Delete a Mailing List

Remove a mailing list card from your address book.

1 Click **Communicator**, **Address Book** to open the Address Book dialog box.

2 Click mailing list name to select it.

3 Press **Delete**.

E-mail: Address an E-mail Message

Select an address from the address book when you are creating, replying to, or forwarding e-mail and group messages.

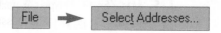

Notes:

- Use this procedure when you want to send an e-mail message and the recipient(s) are listed in your address book.

- For information on adding addresses to the Address Book, see **Address Book: Add Individuals to the Address Book** and **Address Book: Add Mailing Lists to the Address Book**.

- This procedure tells you how to select addresses for a message displayed on your screen. You can also create a new message from within the address book. Open the address book, select the recipient, and press **Ctrl+M**.

1 Display message to address.

2 Click [Address] to open the Select Addresses dialog box.

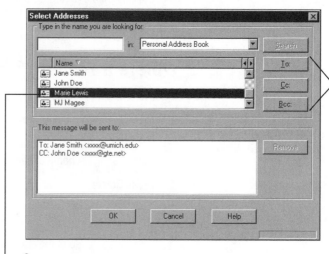

3 Click recipient name to select it.

  *NOTE: To select multiple names, press **Ctrl** and click each name.*

4 Click **To**, **Cc**, or **Bcc** to specify the recipient type. The name is added to the list of recipients at the bottom of the dialog box.

5 Repeat from step 3 to add more recipients as desired.

6 Click [OK].

Notes:

- Recipient types are as follows:

To. Recipients for whom the message is written.

Cc: Carbon copy recipients are those who might be interested in the message.

Bcc: Blind carbon copy recipients receive the message, but are not listed as recipients in the message that others receive (the names of all other recipient types appear in each copy of the message).

Group: Message to post to a discussion group.

Reply-To: Used in mailing lists. If this field appears in a message that you have received from a mailing list, the e-mail address listed here is the appropriate address to reply to if you want to respond to the message. This might be the individual who wrote the message or it might be the address of the entire mailing list.

Followup-To: Used in newsgroup messages to cross-post a message to other groups that are following the message thread. Use with care; avoid flooding groups with irrelevant messages.

Change Recipient Type

When you select recipients from the address book, you can select from only To:, Cc:, or Bcc recipient types. Use this procedure to change the recipient type.

1   Click the recipient type box next to the name of the recipient to change in the message. A list of recipient types opens.

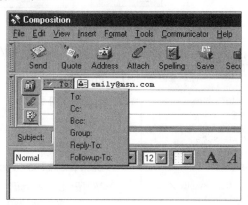

2   Click the new recipient type.

Set Automatic Bcc Recipient Option

1   Click **Edit**, **Preferences**.

2   Click **Messages** (under **Mail & Groups**) in the **Category** list at the left side of the dialog box.

3   Deselect the **Mail Messages: Self** option under **Copies of outgoing messages**.

NOTE: *Enter the address of an automatic Bcc recipient in the Other address option.*

4   Click [OK].

145

E-mail: Create and Send Mail Messages

Create e-mail messages and send them immediately, if working online, or store them to send later in a batch. If you want to save your message to continue working on it later, save it as a draft message.

Message ➡ New Message

Notes:

- You must be in Netscape Messenger to create a mail message. For example, you can be in the Message Center, the Inbox, or Address Book.

- You do not have to be connected to the Internet to create messages. You can work offline while composing messages and then connect to send them.

- If you want to save a message without sending it so that you can work on it later, save it as a draft message.

- Messages waiting to be sent are stored in the Unsent Messages folder. Draft messages are stored in the Draft folder. To edit messages in these folders, see **Email: Edit Draft Messages and Unsent Messages**.

Create an E-Mail Message

1 Press **Ctrl+M** to open the Composition dialog box.

2 Type e-mail address.

OR

Click [Address] to select recipient(s) from the Address Book.

NOTE: See **E-mail: Address an E-mail Message** for detailed information on selecting addresses from the Address Book.

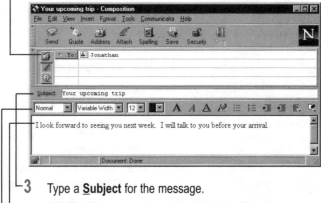

3 Type a **Subject** for the message.

NOTE: Type a concise subject that identifies the message. The Subject field is useful for filing and finding messages at a later date.

4 Type the body of the message.

5 To format text in the body of the message if desired:

a. Drag across text to select it.

b. Click a formatting button. For example, you might underline text, change the font, or add bullets to paragraphs.

- To forward and/or reply to messages that you have received, see **E-mail: Receive and Respond to Messages**.

- For a discussion on e-mail etiquette, see **E-Mail: An Overview**. For ways to convey emotions using emoticons, see **Emoticons and Abbreviations**.

- To automatically add your signature or other information at the end of all messages that you send, see **E-mail: Add a Signature or Other Information to Messages**.

- To create a message while in the address book, select the recipient, and press **Ctrl+M**.

- To create a mail message that includes a hyperlink to the Web page that is currently displayed in the Navigator window, click **File**, **Send Page**. This opens a new message with the hyperlink to the page in the body of the message. This feature makes it easy to send the addresses of interesting pages that you find to your friends.

6 To send a file to the recipient(s) of the e-mail message if desired:

a. Click .

b. Click **File**.

c. Double-click the file to send. The filename is added to the message header.

7 To send or save the message:

- Click or press **Ctrl+S** to save the message as a draft so that you can work on it later. Then, click ⊠ to close the message.

- Click **File**, **Send Later** to send the message to the Unsent Messages folder. It will be sent the next time you send messages.

- Click **File**, **Send Now** to immediately send the message.

Send Unsent Mail

Sends all messages stored in the Unsent Messages folder.

1 Press **Ctrl+2** to go to Messenger Mailbox.

2 Click **File**, **Send Unsent Messages**.

E-mail: Edit Draft Messages and Unsent Messages

When you create a mail message, you have the option of saving it as a draft so that you can continue working on it later. Or you can store it as an unsent message to be sent later in a batch. Use this section to edit or delete these messages.

Notes:

- Messages that you save as drafts are stored in the Drafts folder.

- When you have finished working on a draft message, you can send it immediately or you can move it to the Unsent Messages folder where it will be sent when you next send all mail.

- Messages that you save in order to send later are sent to the Unsent Message folder.

Edit or Delete a Draft Message or an Unsent Message

1 Press **Ctrl+2** to go to the Messenger Mailbox.

2 Click drop-down arrow in **Inbox** to open list of folders.

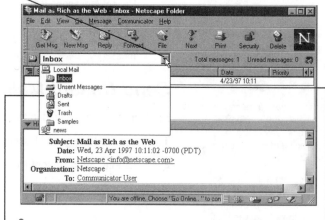

3 To work with a draft message, click the **Drafts** icon.

OR

To work with an unsent message, click the **Unsent Messages** icon.

4 To open and edit a message, double-click the message to open. To save changes that you make, press **Ctrl+S**.

OR

To delete a message, click on the message to select it. Then press **Delete**.

Notes:

• It is recommended that you always spell check your messages before you send them.

Spell Check Message

Use this procedures when working in the mail Composition window.

1 Click .

2 If the speller detects a misspelled word, suggested spelling(s) are listed in the **Suggestions** list. To replace a word:

   a. • Edit the word in the Word box.

      OR

      • Click a word in the **Suggestions** list.

   b. Click [Replace] to change the current occurrence only or click [Replace All] to replace all occurrences of the word in the message.

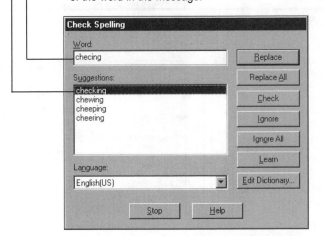

3 To skip the current occurrence of the word, click [Ignore] or to skip all occurrences, click [Ignore All].

4 To replace the current occurrence of the word in the message and also add the word to the dictionary so that it will not be found as a misspelling in the future, click [Learn].

5 To cancel spell checking if desired, click [Stop].

6 Click [Done] when finished spell checking to close the Check Spelling dialog box.

*NOTE: The **Done** button displays in the dialog box when the message has been spell checked.*

E-mail: Filter Incoming Mail

Create filters that set how Netscape Communicator will file messages or otherwise manage incoming mail. For example, if you receive unwelcome messages from a particular sender, you can have Netscape Communicator automatically delete all messages from that sender.

Notes:

- Filters perform actions, such as filing incoming messages in a particular folder. For example, you could have Netscape Communicator automatically file incoming messages in which the message subject contains the text Project X. These messages could be sent to a Project X message folder. For information on creating new message folders, see **E-mail: Organize Messages in Folders**.

- Another way you could use filters is to create a filter that changes the priority of all mail from a particular client to urgent to bring it to your attention.

Create a Filter

1 Press **Ctrl+2** to go to the Inbox or press **Ctrl+Shift+1** to go open the Message Center window.

2 Click **Edit**, **Mail Filters** to open the Mail Filters dialog box. The Mail Filters dialog box lists the filters you have created.

3 Click ⟦ New... ⟧ to open the Filter Rules dialog box.

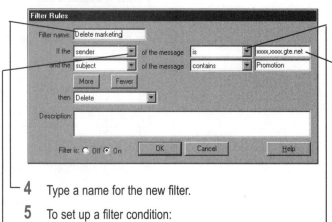

4 Type a name for the new filter.

5 To set up a filter condition:

a. Click drop-down arrow and select the field to use in the condition.

b. Click drop-down arrow and select condition for this field.

NOTE: The available conditions depend on which field is selected.

c. Type or select condition to meet.

d. Click ⟦ More ⟧ to add another field to set up another condition if desired. Repeat from step a. to set up the condition.

NOTE: To delete a condition, click ⟦ Fewer ⟧. This deletes the last condition in the dialog box.

150

6 Click drop-down arrow and select action to take if conditions are met.

*NOTE: If the action is to delete messages, incoming messages meeting the condition(s) in the filter are moved to the Trash folder in the Message Center (**Ctrl+Shift+1**).*

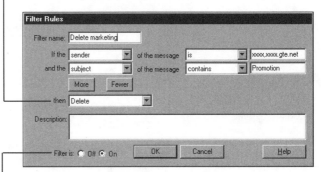

7 Type a **Description** if desired.

8 Click OK .

Temporarily Disable or Enable a Filter

1 Click **Edit**, **Mail Filters** to open the Mail Filters dialog box.

2 Click the filter to disable or enable.

3 Click Edit... .

4 Click **Filter is Off** to disable the filter.

OR

Click **Filter is On** to enable it.

E-mail: Find E-mail Names and Addresses

Use directories on the Internet to locate the e-mail addresses of individuals and businesses. In addition to the directories described here, many search pages also have access to directories for finding e-mail addresses.

Notes:

- The Internet contains a number of directories that you can use to locate people. How successful your search is depends on how much information you can enter in your search criteria to find the person (such as the name, city, etc.). If you do not find the person using a particular directory, try searching another directory.

- You can also search for e-mail names from the Netscape search page. Many search pages have links to one or more pages from which you can search for e-mail addresses.

- You can use this procedure from anywhere in Netscape Navigator or Messenger.

Find an Address on the Internet

1   Click **Edit**, **Search Directory** to display the Search dialog box.

2   Select the directory that you wish to search in the **Search for items** list.

3   Use the fields to enter search criteria.

4   To add or remove fields to use in your search criteria:

- Click **More** to display another field. Each time you click this button, another field is added to the Search dialog box (up to a maximum of five fields).

- Click **Fewer** to remove a field from the Search dialog box. Each time you click the button, another field is removed from the bottom of the dialog box.

- Click the drop-down arrow in a field and select another field to search on.

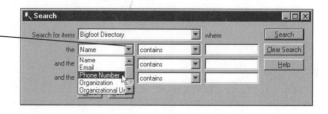

5   Click **Search** to find the name you are looking for.

Notes:

- If your address book is lengthy, use this procedure to quickly go to an address.

Find an Address in the Address Book

1 Click **Communicator**, **Address Book** to open the Address Book dialog box.

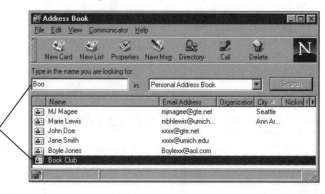

2 Type the name you are searching for. The name is highlighted as soon as you have typed enough characters for Netscape Communicator to identify it.

E-mail: Go to Netscape Messenger

Messenger is the message component of Netscape Communicator. Go to Messenger to send and retrieve e-mail and newsgroup messages.

Communicator ➡ Messenger Mailbox or Message Center

Notes:

- Use this procedure to read and reply to messages and to create new mail without getting new messages on the network. Use this procedure to work offline to read and write mail messages without connecting to the network.

- The Inbox, also called the Messenger Mailbox, lists headers for the messages that you have received in the top pane. The bottom pane shows the text of the selected message.

Go to the Inbox without Getting New Mail

Click **Communicator**, **Messenger Mailbox**.

- The top pane lists message headers. Click a header to view the message body in the bottom pane.

- The bottom pane shows the content of the selected message.

- Click the Hide arrow to close the bottom pane. To reopen the pane, click the arrow again, which appears in the Status bar when the pane is closed.

- Click to view more message header fields or click to remove fields.

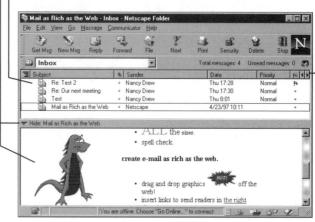

Notes:

- If you are working online, gets new mail. If you are offline, allows you to connect to the network and then downloads mail.

- If the Component Bar is docked, the Mailbox button will be on right side of the window in the status bar.

Go to the Inbox and Get New Mail

Click [Mailbox] on the Component bar.

154

Notes:

- From the Message Center you can access stored mail messages, including drafts that you are working on, messages in the Inbox, and copies of messages that you have sent. You can view, edit, and delete messages by opening folders and messages. To create message folders and file messages, see **E-mail: Organize Messages in Folders**.

- The Message Center stores local mail. Local mail is stored on your hard disk (rather than on a mail server). Communicator downloads your new messages into the Message Center. To download new messages, follow **Go to the Inbox and Get New Mail** procedure on the previous page.

- You can also create messages from the Message Center.

Go to the Message Center

Click **Communicator**, **Message Center**. The Netscape Message Center window opens.

E-mail: Organize Messages in Folders

The Message Center stores e-mail and newsgroup messages. Go to the Message Center to create folders to organize mail that you want to file.

Notes:

- Local mail refers to messages located on your hard disk. These include messages that you have created but not yet sent (Unsent Messages folder), draft messages that you are working on (Drafts folder), copies of mail that you have sent (Sent folder), and messages that you have received (Inbox folder).

- To open a folder to display messages, double-click the folder. You can browse through message headers and open and edit messages.

Go to the Message Center

1 Click **Communicator**, **Message Center** to open the Message Center window.

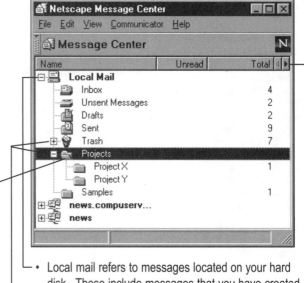

- Local mail refers to messages located on your hard disk. These include messages that you have created but not yet sent (Unsent Messages folder), draft messages that you are working on (Drafts folder), copies of mail that you have sent (Sent folder), and messages that you have received (Inbox folder).

- To display subfolders within a folder, click ⊞. To close a folder, click ⊟.

- Create message folders to organize messages, such as the Projects folder in the illustration. See **Create a Folder to Store Messages** on the following page.

- Click ◀ to view more fields or click ▶ to remove fields in the window. (For example, "Unread" is a field.)

Create a Folder to Store Messages

1 Click **File**, **New Folder** to open the New Folder dialog box.

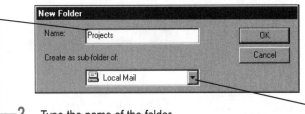

2 Type the name of the folder.

3 Click the drop-down arrow and select the folder in which to create the new folder.

4 Click OK .

File a Message in a Folder

1 Double-click the folder containing the message in the Message Center window.

2 Right-click the message.

3 Click **File Message** and then click the folder in which to file the message.

Rename a Folder

1 Right-click the folder to rename in the Message Center window.

2 Click **Rename Folder**.

3 Type new name and click OK .

E-mail: Receive and Respond to Messages

Download new messages into your Inbox. This procedure also includes procedures to reply to and forward the messages you have retrieved.

File ➡ Get Messages

Notes:

- If you are working online, this procedure gets new mail immediately. If you are offline, it allows you to connect to the network and then downloads mail.

- If the Component Bar is docked, the Mailbox button will be on the right side of the window in the status bar.

Get New Mail

- From another Netscape Communicator component

  (such as Navigator), click [Mailbox] on the Component Bar to switch to the Inbox and get new mail.
- From within Messenger, press **Ctrl+T**.

Notes:

- Messages that you receive are stored in the Inbox.

Open a Message

1 Press **Ctrl+2** to go to the Inbox.

2 Double-click the message to open.

Notes:

- Bcc (blind carbon copy) recipients automatically receive copies of replies. Bcc recipients do not appear in the message header.

Reply to a Message

1 Open the message.

2 To reply to the sender of the message only, press **Ctrl+R**.

OR

To reply to the sender and all other recipients of the original message, press **Ctrl+Shift+R**.

NOTE: By default, Netscape Communicator includes the text of the message to which you are responding in your reply. If you have disabled this setting, you can include the text of the original message by clicking **File**, **Quote Original Text**.

158

3 Type message.

4 To send or save the message:

• Press **Ctrl+S** to save the message as a draft so that you can work on it later. Then, click ☒ to close the message.

• Click **File**, **Send Later** to send the message to Unsent Messages. The message will be sent the next time you send unsent messages.

• Click **File**, **Send Now** to immediately send the message.

Forward a Message

Send a message you have received to another e-mail recipient.

1 Open the message to forward.

2 Click [Forward] or press **Ctrl+L** to send the text of the original message as a file attachment.

OR

Press **Ctrl+Shift+L** to send the text of the original message in the body of the current message.

3 Type your message if desired.

4 To send or save the message:

• Press **Ctrl+S** to save the message as a draft so that you can work on it later. Then, click ☒ to close the message.

• Click **File**, **Send Later** to send the message to Unsent Messages. The message will be sent the next time you send unsent messages.

• Click **File**, **Send Now** to immediately send the message.

E-mail: Search Messages

You can quickly locate e-mail messages by searching through them. You can search messages displayed in the Message Center window.

Notes:

- You can search all mail folders or a particular folder including any subfolders.

Search E-mail Messages

1   Click **Communicator**, **Message Center**.

2   Click **Edit**, **Search Messages** to display the Search Messages dialog box.

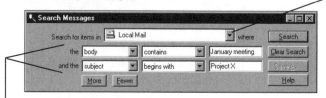

3   Click the **Search for items in** drop-down arrow and select the folder or discussion group to search.

NOTE: If you select Local Mail, Netscape Communicator searches all mail message folders.

4   Use the fields to enter search criteria.

5   To add or remove search criteria fields if desired:

- Click **More** to add another search criteria field. Each time you click the button, another field is added to the Search Messages dialog box (up to a maximum of five fields).

- Click **Fewer** to remove a field. Each time you click the button, a field is removed from the bottom of the dialog box.

6 Click a 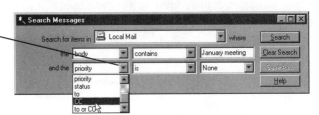 drop-down arrow next to a field and select a different field to search on if desired.

7 Click the drop-down arrow in the condition field to select a different condition if desired.

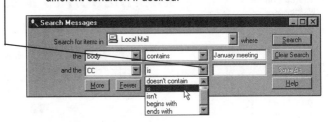

8 Click Search.

NOTE: If you were unable to find the message, click the *Clear Search* *button to set up a different search.*

E-mail: Set Outgoing Message Formatting Preferences

Set the formatting of the original text in messages that you reply to or forward, automatically add your signature at the end of all outgoing messages, or add information about yourself such as your company name at the end of messages.

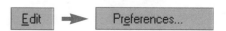

Notes:

- You can have Netscape Communicator automatically include your name or other signature at the end of messages that you send. The signature must be located in a plain-text file on disk. Netscape Communicator adds the message from the file for each message that you send.

- You can also enter information about yourself, such as a company name or an address, in the Personal Address Card and Netscape Communicator will append the information to the end of all messages that you send.

- Edit the information in your Personal Card by clicking the **Edit Card** button in the Preferences dialog box.

Add a Signature or Other Information to Messages

1 Click **Edit**, **Preferences**.

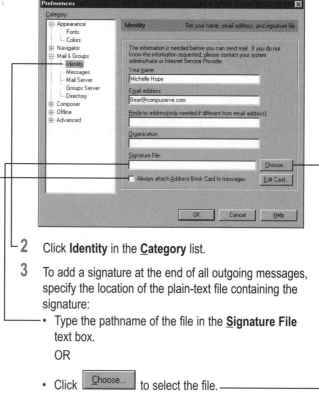

2 Click **Identity** in the **Category** list.

3 To add a signature at the end of all outgoing messages, specify the location of the plain-text file containing the signature:

- Type the pathname of the file in the **Signature File** text box.

  OR

- Click Choose... to select the file.

4 To add information about yourself at the end of all outgoing messages:

  a. Select the **Always attach Address Book Card to messages** check box.

  b. Click Create Card at the prompt (prompt appears if you have not yet created a Personal Card).

c. Enter information about yourself that you would like to include at the end of your messages.

d. Click ▭ OK ▭.

5 Click ▭ OK ▭ to close the Preferences dialog box.

Format Original Message Text in Messages that you Reply To

1 Click **Edit**, **Preferences**.

2 Click **Mail & Groups** in the **Category** list.

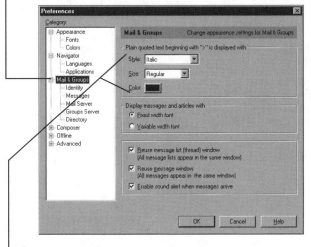

3 Set **Style**, **Size**, and **Color** options.

4 Click ▭ OK ▭.

163

Navigator: Bookmarks Window

Open the Bookmarks window to view the structure of the Bookmarks menu. For information on using the Bookmarks window to organize bookmarks on the Bookmarks menu, see **Navigator: Customize the Bookmarks Menu**.

Notes:

- When you first open the Bookmarks window it displays bookmarks and folders. You can also display fields for the address of the bookmarked page, when you last visited it, and the date on which you created the bookmark.

- You can move the fields in the window in any order.

Work in the Bookmarks Window

1 Press **Ctrl+B** to open the Bookmarks window.

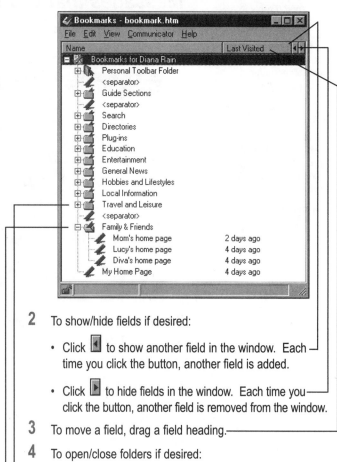

2 To show/hide fields if desired:

- Click ◄ to show another field in the window. Each time you click the button, another field is added.

- Click ► to hide fields in the window. Each time you click the button, another field is removed from the window.

3 To move a field, drag a field heading.

4 To open/close folders if desired:

- Click ⊞ (the plus sign) next to a closed folder to open it and display the bookmarks and/or subfolders contained within it.

- Click ⊟ (the minus sign) next to an open folder to close it.

5 To sort bookmarks in the Bookmarks window, if desired:

a. Click **View** to open the View menu.

b. Click the field to sort on.

5 Click when finished to close the window.

Notes:

- Use this procedure to have Netscape Communicator check to see if a bookmarked page has changed since you last visited it. You can check all bookmarked pages or selected bookmarks.

Check for Changed Pages

1 Click bookmark to check individual page(s) if desired.

*NOTE: To select multiple bookmarks, press **Ctrl** and click pages.*

2 Click **View**, **Update Bookmarks**. The What's New dialog box displays.

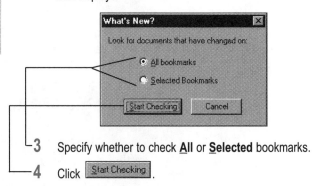

3 Specify whether to check **All** or **Selected** bookmarks.

4 Click [Start Checking].

165

Navigator: Create Bookmarks

Bookmarks mark the location of your favorite Web pages. When you create a bookmark for an Internet site, Netscape Communicator adds it to the Bookmarks menu. To quickly jump to the page, simply select the site from the menu.

Communicator ➡ Bookmarks ➡ Add Bookmark

Notes:

- After adding a bookmark you can move it to another folder. See **Navigator: Customize the Bookmarks Menu** for procedures on organizing bookmarks in folders.

Adding Bookmarks

When you create a bookmark, you can add it as a command on the Bookmark menu or as a subcommand stored in a subfolder.

When you add a bookmark using the Add Bookmark command, the page name for the bookmark appears directly on the Bookmarks menu.

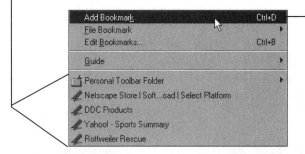

When you add a bookmark using the **File Bookmark** command, the bookmark is placed in a subfolder that you select, and its page name appears on a submenu in the Bookmarks menu.

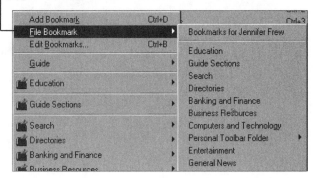

166

Create a Bookmark and Add It to the Bookmark Menu

This procedure adds the bookmark to the bottom of the Bookmarks menu.

1 Display the page for which you will create a bookmark.

2 Press **Ctrl+D**.

Create a Bookmark and Add It to a Bookmark Submenu

This procedure adds a bookmark as a subcommand by placing it in a subfolder. See **Adding Bookmarks** in this section for an illustration of this.

1 Display the page for which you will create a bookmark.

2 Click **Communicator**, **Bookmarks**, **File Bookmark**.

3 Click the subfolder in which to store the bookmark.

Create a Bookmark to a Site in History List

This procedure adds a bookmark to the bottom of the Bookmark menu. To move the bookmark to a subfolder, see **Navigator: Customize the Bookmarks Menu**.

1 Press **Ctrl+H** to open the History list.

2 Right-click the page to mark and click **Add to Bookmarks**.

3 Press **Ctrl+W** to close the History list.

Go to a Bookmarked Page

Use this procedure while you are online to jump to a page marked with a bookmark.

1 Click ![Bookmarks] on Location toolbar.

2 Click folder name containing bookmark as necessary.

3 Click bookmark name.

167

Navigator: Customize Bookmarks Menu

Organize the Bookmarks menu so that you can easily locate bookmarks when you are navigating the Internet. Move bookmarks to different folders, rename, delete, and otherwise organize items on the Bookmarks menu.

Communicator ➡ Bookmarks ➡ Edit Bookmarks...

Notes:

- Create folders to hold bookmarks and to organize bookmarks in categories. For example, you might have a Family and Friends folder, a Project X folder, or any other category. Folders appear as submenus on the Bookmarks menu. See **Adding Bookmarks** in **Navigator: Create Bookmarks** for an illustration of how folders appear on the Bookmarks menu.

- You can create subfolders within folders.

- For an overview of working in the Bookmarks window, see **Navigator: Bookmarks Window**.

Create a Folder

1 Press **Ctrl+B** to open the Bookmarks window.

2 Click folder to contain subfolder.

3 Click **File, New Folder**.

4 Type descriptive **Name** for folder.

5 Type a **Description** if desired.

6 Click [OK].

7 Click ⊠ when finished to close Bookmarks window.

Move a Bookmark to a Different Folder

Move bookmarks between folders to organize them in categories.

1 Press **Ctrl+B** to open the Bookmarks window.

2 Drag bookmark to new location.

3 Click ⊠ when finished to close Bookmarks window.

Delete a Bookmark or Folder

1 Press **Ctrl+B** to open the Bookmarks window.

2 Click item to delete.

3 Press **Delete** key.

4 Click ⊠ when finished to close Bookmarks window.

Rename a Bookmark or Folder

1 Press **Ctrl+B** to open the Bookmarks window.

2 Right-click the item to rename.

3 Click **Bookmark Properties**.

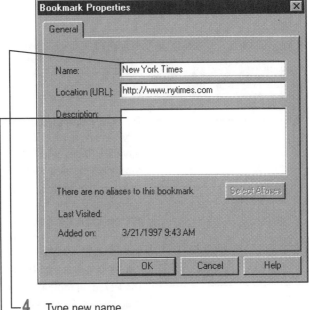

4 Type new name.

5 Type a description if desired.

6 Click OK .

7 Click ⊠ when finished to close Bookmarks window.

Navigator: Customize Navigator Toolbars

You can change the appearance of the Navigation and Personal toolbars or hide them to use the entire window to view a page.

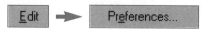

Notes:

• See also **Navigator: Customize Personal Toolbar** for procedures on setting up your own toolbar with buttons to jump to sites that you often visit.

Navigator Toolbars

Three toolbars are available when you are navigating the Web. These are the Navigation toolbar, the Location toolbar, and the Personal toolbar.

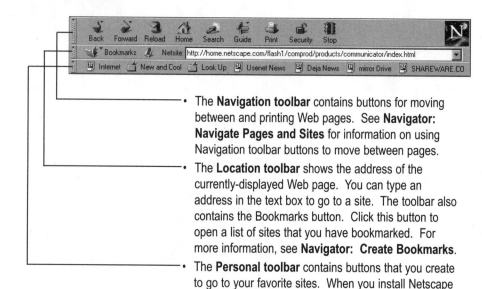

• The **Navigation toolbar** contains buttons for moving between and printing Web pages. See **Navigator: Navigate Pages and Sites** for information on using Navigation toolbar buttons to move between pages.

• The **Location toolbar** shows the address of the currently-displayed Web page. You can type an address in the text box to go to a site. The toolbar also contains the Bookmarks button. Click this button to open a list of sites that you have bookmarked. For more information, see **Navigator: Create Bookmarks**.

• The **Personal toolbar** contains buttons that you create to go to your favorite sites. When you install Netscape Communicator, the Internet, New and Cool, and Lookup buttons are on the Personal toolbar. These buttons take you to Netscape guides such as sites where you can locate people in the Yellow Pages or visit the newest sites on the Web. For more information, see **Navigator: Netscape Guides**. You can delete these buttons to add your own favorite sites since these sites can be accessed through menus. See the next section, **Navigator: Customize Personal Toolbar**.

Notes:

- Settings apply to buttons on the Navigation toolbar and the Personal toolbar.

Show Text/Graphics on Toolbars

Show text only, graphics only, or graphics and text on toolbar buttons.

1 Click **Edit**, **Preferences** to display the Preferences dialog box.

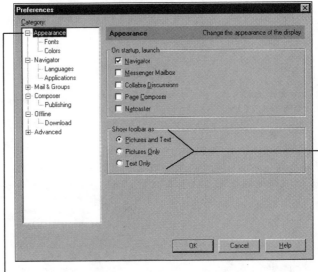

2 Click **Appearance** in the **Category** list.

3 Click a **Show toolbar as** option to set the button display.

4 Click ___OK___.

Show/Hide Toolbars

1 Click **View**.

2 Select toolbar to show or hide:
- Click **Navigation Toolbar**.
- Click **Location Toolbar**.
- Click **Personal Toolbar**.

Notes:

- Use the same procedure to show or hide toolbars.

- Hide toolbars to view more of the currently-displayed page. You can then show them again when you need to use them.

Navigator: Customize Personal Toolbar

The Personal toolbar is completely customizable—for example, you can add buttons that jump to your favorite Web sites. The toolbar comes with three preset buttons which you can remove to make room for your own buttons.

Communicator → Bookmarks → 📁 Personal Toolbar Folder

Notes:

- Shortcuts on the Personal toolbar are stored in the Personal Toolbar folder. You work with the contents of this folder in the Bookmarks window.

- You must open the Personal Toolbar folder in order to remove, rename, or reorder buttons on the Personal toolbar.

- Shortcuts that are stored in subfolders of the Personal Toolbar folder are available on the Personal toolbar. The toolbar button name is the folder name. Clicking the button opens a list of the shortcuts (or other subfolders) contained in the folder. The **New and Cool** button (a default button on the Personal toolbar when you install Netscape Communicator) is an example of how subfolders work.

Open the Personal Toolbar Folder

1 Press **Ctrl+B** to open the Bookmarks window.

2 Click **Personal Toolbar Folder**.

 NOTE: If the Personal Toolbar folder is closed, click the plus sign (⊞) next to it to open it.

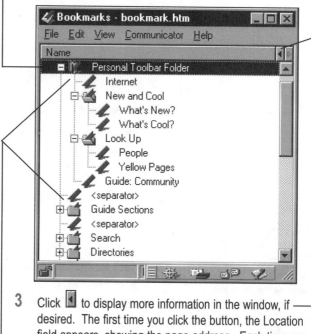

3 Click ◀ to display more information in the window, if desired. The first time you click the button, the Location field appears, showing the page address. Each time you click the arrow, more information appears.

 NOTE: Buttons and subfolders that appear on the Personal toolbar are all located in the Personal Toolbar folder.

Notes:

- You can create the shortcut to the Web page as a button on the Personal toolbar. Or, place it in a subfolder in the Personal Toolbar folder to add it as a command on the drop-down menu that appears when you click a button on the Personal toolbar.

Create a Button that Jumps to the Displayed Web Page

1   Display page for which to create button.

2   Drag on the Location toolbar to the Personal toolbar. A new button is created for the page.

OR

Click **Communicator**, **Bookmarks**, **File Bookmark**, **Personal Toolbar Folder**, **Personal Toolbar Folder** and then the subfolder in which to create the shortcut.

Arrange Buttons and Commands on the Personal Toolbar

1   **Open the Personal Toolbar Folder** (follow procedure on previous page).

2   To create a subfolder if desired:

    a. Click folder to contain subfolder.

    b. Click **File**, **New Folder**.

    c. Type descriptive **Name** for folder.

    d. Type a **Description** if desired.

    e. Click [OK].

3   To move a shortcut if desired:

    Drag shortcut to new location within Personal Toolbar folder.

4   To delete a shortcut or folder if desired:

    a. Click folder or shortcut to delete.

    b. Press **Delete key**.

5   Click when finished to close Bookmarks window.

Navigator: Disable Graphics

If speed is more important to you than viewing graphics on Web pages, navigating the Internet is much faster if you turn off the graphic display. Use this procedure to view text only or to include both text and graphics on Web pages.

Notes:

- Because Netscape Communicator does not have to load graphics, which require more resources, pages will open much faster when you disable graphics. Part of the fun of exploring the Internet is the graphic elements on Web pages, but they can really slow you down. When you want to quickly find information, disable graphics.

- Graphics on Web pages are replaced by placeholders when you disable graphics.

- You can perform this procedure while you are working online. If graphics are disabled and you want to see all of the graphics on the current page, enable pictures and then reload the page.

- To view a particular graphic on a page without enabling all graphics, see **View a Graphic in Text-Only Mode** on the next page.

Enable or Disable Graphics

1 Click **Edit**, **Preferences**.

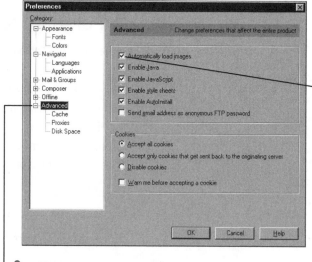

2 Click **Advanced** in the **Category** list.

3 Select or deselect **Automatically load images**.

   NOTE: When the option is selected, Netscape Communicator displays text and pictures. Clearing the option displays text only.

4 Click [OK].

5 Click [Reload] or press **Ctrl+R** to update the currently displayed Web page to the new setting if desired.

   NOTE: If Navigator has already loaded graphics for the page, it will display them even when in text-only mode. This is because it does not take any more time to display graphics since they are already downloaded.

Notes:

- Use this procedure to view an individual graphic on a page without enabling all graphics. Netscape Communicator loads just the graphic that you specify.

View a Graphic in Text-Only Mode

1 Right-click the graphic placeholder to open the shortcut menu.

NOTE: *The above illustration shows the shortcut menu that appears if the graphic is a hyperlink (jumps to a different location when you click it). If the graphic is a picture on the page, the shortcut menu will not include link commands.*

2 Click **Show Image**. Navigator loads the graphic.

Notes:

- Use this procedure to display all graphics on the current page only without enabling graphics.

- The Images button is available on the toolbar only when graphics are disabled.

View All Graphics on a Page in Text-Only Mode

Click .

OR

Click **View, Show Images**.

Navigator: History List

The History List is a list that Netscape keeps of sites you have previously visited. You can use the History list to browse sites and find the address of a page that you would like to revisit.

Notes:

- From the History window, you can go directly to a site that you have previously visited.

- By default, Netscape Communicator stores sites in the history list for nine days. See **Set Number of Days to Store History List Entries** on the next page if you would like to change the length of time that Netscape Communicator stores sites in the History List.

- To sort the list on a different field, click the **View** menu and select a sort field.

- To search for a particular page in the list, click **Edit**, **Search History List**.

Work in the History Window

1 Press **Ctrl+H** to open the History window.

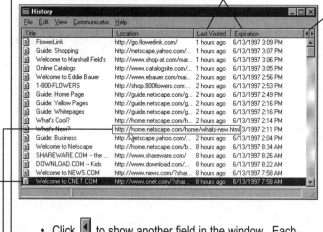

- Click ◀ to show another field in the window. Each time you click the button, another field is added.

- Click ▶ to hide fields in the window. Each time you click the button, another field is removed.

- To move a field, drag a field heading to a new position.

- To view the entire field entry in a pop-up box, place mouse pointer over desired field entry.

- To select an address, click on it. To go to a site, double-click.

2 To close the History window, press **Ctrl+W**.

Notes:

- Copy the address and paste it somewhere else, such as in an e-mail message. This procedure copies only the address and not the other fields, such as the site name.

Notes:

- By default, Netscape Communicator deletes addresses in the history list after nine days. Use this procedure to change the length of time that addresses are stored.

Copy a Page Address

1 Press **Ctrl+H** to open the History window.

2 Click on the site to copy.

3 Press **Ctrl+C** to copy the address.

4 Switch to message or other document in which to place address.

5 Press **Ctrl+V** to paste the address.

Set Number of Days to Store History List Entries

1 Click **E̲dit**, **Pr̲eferences**.

2 Click **Navigator** in the **C̲ategory** list.

3 Click **Pages in History ex̲pire after**.

4 Type number of days to store addresses in text box.

5 Click [OK].

Delete all History Entries

Erases all entries in the history list.

1 Click **E̲dit**, **Pr̲eferences**.

2 Click **Navigator** in the **C̲ategory** list.

3 Click [Clea̲r History].

4 Click [OK].

Navigator: Home Page

The home page is the page that opens when you click the Home button. The default home page is the Netscape home page.

Notes:

- You can change the home page while you are connected to the Internet or while working offline.

- By default, the start page is set to the home page. The start page is the page that Netscape Communicator opens each time you start the program and connect to the Internet. To change the start page, see **Start Page**.

- The term "home page" also refers to the page that you create about yourself and publish on the Web.

Change the Home Page

1 Click **Edit**, **Preferences**.

> *NOTE: To have Netscape Communicator automatically change the home page to the address of a particular page, first display the page.*

2 Click **Navigator** in the **Category** list.

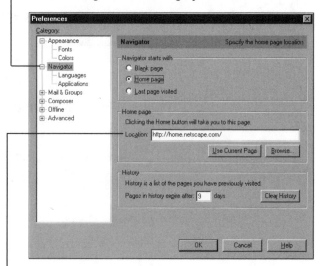

3 Choose one of the following methods to enter the address of the new home page:

- Type the page address in the **Location** text box.

- Click **Use Current Page** to enter the address of the currently displayed page.

- Click **Browse...** to locate a page address. Double-click the address to enter in the **Location** text box.

4 Click **OK**.

178

Go to the Home Page

Click or click **Go**, **Home**.

The Netscape Home Page (default)

• Click a button to go to other pages in the Netscape
  site. Scroll to the bottom of the page for more pages
  you can visit.

• Today's date. The page is updated daily.

• Netscape announcements and information about the
  company.

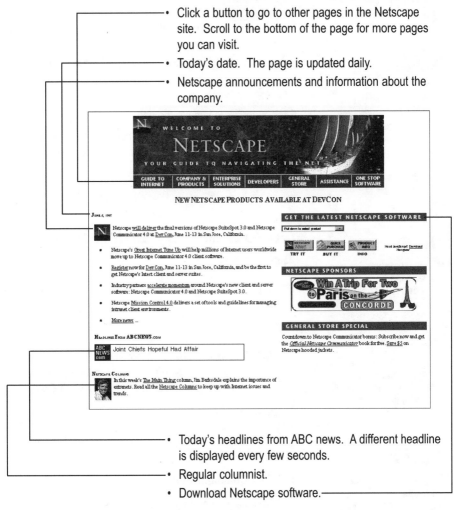

• Today's headlines from ABC news. A different headline
  is displayed every few seconds.

• Regular columnist.

• Download Netscape software.

Move between pages while you are connected to the Internet. Go to different pages in a single site or go to a another site, including sites that you have previously visited.

Cancel a Jump

Click ____ or press **Esc**.

Go to a Site by Selecting a Hyperlink

Click hyperlink to jump to the page.

> NOTE: When you move the mouse pointer over a hyperlink, the pointer looks like: 🖑 .

Go to a Site By Entering an Address

1 Type the address of the site to go to in the **Location** text box.

`Bookmarks` `Location:` `http://www.netscape.com`

> NOTE: The text box is located in the Location toolbar. When you type an address in the Location text box, the name of the text changes to **Go to**.

2 Press **Enter**.

Go to Recently Visited Page

1 Click **Communicator**.

2 Click page to go to (at bottom of menu).

Go to a Previously Visited Page

1 Press **Ctrl+H** to open the History window.

2 Double-click the page to go to.

Go to a Bookmarked Page

1 Click .

2 Click folder name containing bookmark if necessary.

3 Click page name.

Go to the Search Page

Click or click **Edit**, **Search Internet**.

Go to the Home Page

Click Home or click **Go**, **Home**.

Go to a Netscape Guide

1 Click .

2 Click the guide to go to.

Navigator: Netscape Guides

Netscape provides a number of guides that you can use to browse information on the Web. Each guide is a Web site where you can browse information by category. For example, from the What's New guide you can visit the latest sites on the Web.

Notes:

• You can go to any Netscape guide from the Guide to the Internet page (click **The Internet** in step 2). Or, go straight to a guide such as the newest and coolest pages on the Web, and other guides.

Go to a Netscape Guide

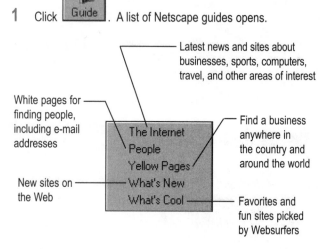

1 Click **Guide**. A list of Netscape guides opens.

Latest news and sites about businesses, sports, computers, travel, and other areas of interest

White pages for finding people, including e-mail addresses

Find a business anywhere in the country and around the world

New sites on the Web

Favorites and fun sites picked by Websurfers

2 Click the Guide site to go to.

Notes:

- The Guide to the Internet page is a good source of news headlines. You can read the latest news in various topics of interest such as business, sports, general news, etc.

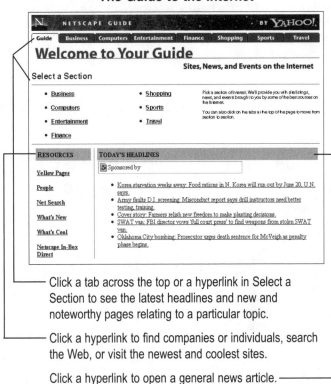

Click a tab across the top or a hyperlink in Select a Section to see the latest headlines and new and noteworthy pages relating to a particular topic.

Click a hyperlink to find companies or individuals, search the Web, or visit the newest and coolest sites.

Click a hyperlink to open a general news article.

Navigator: Netscape Net Search Page

Netscape provides the Netscape Net Search page from which you can search the Web for information. This section shows you how to use and customize the Netscape Net Search page.

Edit ➡ Search Internet

Notes:

- Use Netscape Net Search to search the Web for information and to connect to interesting sites. You can search for specific topics using different search engines. Or, browse through categories of topics or go to a Netscape Guide to find information of interest.

- Click **Edit**, **Search Internet** to display the Netscape Net Search page.

- From the Netscape search page, you can perform your search using different search engines without actually going to the corresponding search page. A search engine is the software that a particular search page uses to find information on the Web. A search page is the Web page that is displayed. For example, if you use Infoseek (as shown in the illustration), the Infoseek search page is not displayed. Navigator sends your search to the Infoseek search engine and displays the results.

Use the Netscape Net Search Page

- Click a tab to use a different search engine.

- Jump to a page in the selected search engine (Infoseek in the example) or search for a topic on the Web using the search engine.

- Add a search tool to this tab and set the default search engine.

- Access more search pages.

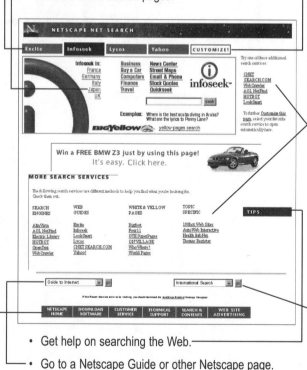

- Get help on searching the Web.

- Go to a Netscape Guide or other Netscape page.

- Search sites in a specific country.

- Information on Netscape products and services.

- Some of the popular search pages that you can go to from the Netscape Net Search page are described in this guide. See **Search Pages: An Overview** for general information on using search pages to find information on the Internet.

- The Netscape Net Search page lists popular search engines on tabs across the top of the page. By default, there are four search engines: Excite, Infoseek, Lycos, and Yahoo. You can add a favorite search engine to the CUSTOMIZE! tab when you first access the page. For example, you might want the fifth tab to go to Webcrawler.

- Each time you open the Netscape Net Search page, a different search engine is highlighted. For example, the first time you open the page, Excite is the default search engine, the second time it is Infoseek, and so on. You can use this procedure to always open to a particular search engine. For example, you might want Metacrawler to the fifth tab and always open to Metacrawler.

Customize the Netscape Search Page

1 Click **Edit**, **Search Internet** to display the Netscape Net Search page.

2 Click **CUSTOMIZE!** (fifth tab located at top of page). The Customize dialog box opens.

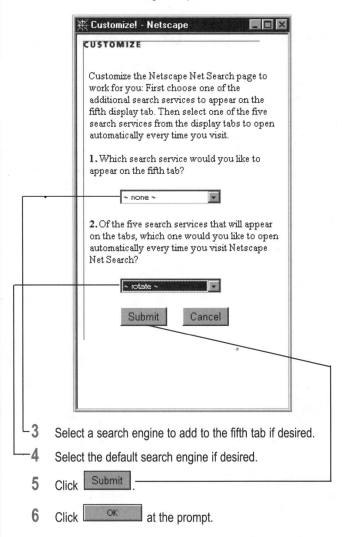

3 Select a search engine to add to the fifth tab if desired.

4 Select the default search engine if desired.

5 Click **Submit**.

6 Click **OK** at the prompt.

Navigator: Search Pages

A search page is a Web page that you go to in order to find information on the Internet. Netscape Navigator comes with bookmarks that you can use to jump to a number of popular search pages, including the Netscape Net Search page described on the previous page.

Notes:

- From the Netscape search page, you can find specific information on the Internet. You can use the Netscape search engine or click hyperlinks to access popular search pages such as Yahoo, Lycos, InfoSeek and many others.

- Some of the popular search pages that you can go to are described in this guide. See **Search Pages: An Overview** for general information on using search pages to find information on the Internet.

- The Netscape search page is customizable. See **Navigator: Netscape Net Search Page** for more information.

Notes:

- The Bookmarks menu contains a list of popular search pages. You can add your favorite search pages to the Bookmarks menu. See **Navigator: Create Bookmarks**.

Go to the Netscape Search Page

Click .

Go to Popular Search Pages

The search pages listed in the Bookmarks menu are also available from the Netscape Net Search Page described in the section called **Search Page: Netscape Net Search Page**.

For a description of some of the popular search pages, see the **Getting Started** section of this book.

1 Click **Communicator**, **Bookmarks**.

2 Click the **Search** folder to open a list of search pages.

3 Click the search page to go to.

Go to the Netscape Guide to the Internet

Click on the Personal toolbar.

> *NOTE: If you removed the Internet button from the Personal toolbar, you can open the Internet guide by clicking*
>
> *and selecting **The Internet** in the drop-down list.*

Find People on the Internet

1 Click  on the Personal toolbar.

2 Click **People**.

Go to the Yellow Pages to Search for Businesses

1 Click Guide .

2 Click **Yellow Pages**.

Navigator: Start Page

The start page is the page that opens each time you start Netscape Navigator. The default start page is the home page. This section tells you how to open to a different page at startup.

Notes:

- If you typically go to a different page each time you go online, you can set the start page to a blank page. When you start Netscape Communicator, it does not display any page.

- See also **Create a Shortcut to Open to a Different Page** on the next page for another way to display different pages when you start Netscape Communicator.

Change the Start Page

1 Click **Edit**, **Preferences**.

2 Click **Navigator** in the **Category** list to display Navigator preferences.

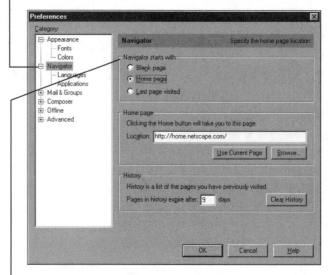

3 Click a **Navigator starts with** option to set the start page:
   - **Blank page** does not open a page at startup.
   - **Home page** displays the Netscape home page (default setting) or other home page that you specified using the **Change the Home Page** procedure in this section.
   - **Last page visited** displays the page that was displayed the last time you exited Netscape Communicator.

4 Click [OK].

Notes:

- Starting Netscape Communicator from a shortcut opens the page specified in the shortcut.

- You can create as many shortcuts as you would like to start Netscape Communicator and open to different pages. For example, create a shortcut to a site that you often visit or create a shortcut to a favorite search page.

- To rename a shortcut, right-click the shortcut and click **Rename**.

Create a Shortcut to Open a Different Page

To have Navigator create the shortcut for you:

1 Display the page for which to create the shortcut.

2 Right-click on the page background to open the shortcut menu for the page.

3 Click **Create Shortcut**.

To create the shortcut if you know the page address:

1 Right-click the Windows desktop.

2 Click **New, Shortcut**. The Create Shortcut dialog box displays.

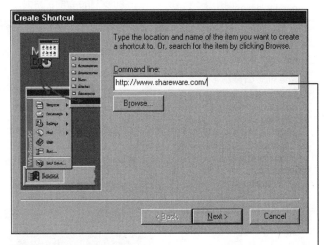

3 Type the page address.

4 Click **Next >**.

5 Type a name for the shortcut and click **Finish**.

Navigator: Work with Information on a Web Page

View Web pages that you have visited, copy information from a page, convert the page to an HTML document, find text on a page, and print a page.

Notes:

• You cannot paste into another Web page.

Copy From a Web Page to a Document

1 To select information to copy, drag across text.

OR

To select the entire page, press **Ctrl+A**.

2 Press **Ctrl+C** to copy the selection.

3 Switch to the document to contain the information.

NOTE: Start up your word processor or other program if necessary and open a document in which to paste the information.

4 Press **Ctrl+V** to paste the information into the document.

Notes:

• Search for a word or phrase on the currently displayed page.

Search the Current Page for Information

1 Press **Ctrl+F** to display the Find dialog box.

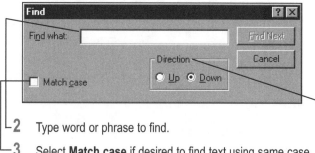

2 Type word or phrase to find.

3 Select **Match case** if desired to find text using same case as that typed in the **Find what** text box. Or deselect the option to find any text that matches, regardless of case.

4 Click a **Direction** option, if desired, to reverse the direction in which Netscape Communicator searches for the text.

5 Click [Find Next] to locate next instance of text in document.

6 Repeat step 5 as desired.

7 Press [Cancel] to close the Find dialog box when finished.

Print a Page

1 Display page to print.

2 Click [Print].

3 Fill out options in the Print dialog box.

4 Click [OK] to print.

Save a Page in an HTML File

Save the text in a Web page in a separate file.

1 Display page to save.

2 Click **File**, **Save As**.

3 Type a **File name** for the file.

4 Click [Save].

Save Graphic in GIF File

1 Right-click an image on a page.

2 Click **Save Image As**.

3 Type a **File name** for the file.

4 Click [Save].

191

Newsgroups: Add a Group Server

Before you can subscribe to discussion groups, you must add the group server in Netscape Communicator. A group server is a computer that stores newsgroup discussions. After you add the server, Netscape Communicator can access it and display the groups on the server.

Notes:

- Use this procedure to set up your first group server. If you need to set up additional servers, use the procedure on the following page.

- In order to subscribe to a discussion group, you must first know the name of the group server. For example, the CompuServe newsgroup server is *news.compuserve.com*. Check your service provider for the name of your group server. Or, if you subscribe to a news service such as ClariNet, they will provide you with the group server name. Some providers offer ClariNet as part of their service package.

Add the Default Group Server

1 Click **Edit**, **Preferences**.

2 Click the plus sign (⊞) next to Mail & Groups in the **Categories** list to show mail and group preferences (if necessary).

3 Click **Groups Server** in the **Category** list.

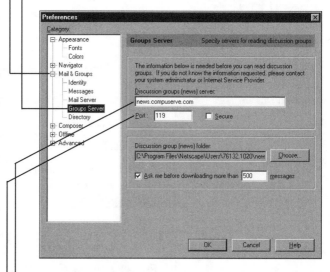

3 Type the name of the server.

4 Type the port number if it is a different port than the default, 119.

> *NOTE: Most discussion group servers use port 119 to receive requests. Change this only if your service provider uses a different port. If you do not know the port number, try using the default. It will probably work. (The port is communications hardware located on the server and is used to send and receive data from your computer. Since computers have multiple ports, you need to identify the correct one.)*

5 Click OK.

Notes:

- Use this procedure if you subscribe to newsgroups on multiple group servers.

Add an Additional Group Server

1 Press **Ctrl+Shift+1** to open the Message Center window.

2 Click **File**, **New Discussion Group Server**.

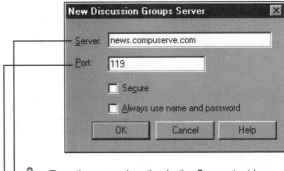

3 Type the server location in the **Server** text box.

4 Type the port number if it is a different port than the default, 119.

NOTE: *Most discussion group servers use port 119 to receive requests. Change this only if your service provider uses a different port. If you do not know the port number, try using the default.*

5 Click **Secure** if desired to send and receive encrypted messages and to require certificates when using newsgroups.

NOTE: *When you use encryption, Communicator codes your messages so that they cannot be read as they pass from computer to computer on the network before they end up at the group server. When the message reaches the group server, it is decrypted. This prevents anyone at intermediary servers from accessing information about you. If you require certificates then you must provide a personal certificate that identifies you on the Internet. You need to apply for this certificate from an Internet site that issues certificates. The group server must provide you with a site certificate that identifies it.*

6 Click **Always use name and password** if desired if you want to require your password when you connect to a newsgroup server. Communicator will display a dialog box for your name and password. Use this option if you want to make sure that nobody else can access newsgroups and post messages in your name without your knowledge.

7 Click OK.

Newsgroups: Remove Old Messages

Downloaded messages can take up disk space, particularly if you download both message header and message text. This section tells you how to automatically delete old messages. By default, Netscape Communicator does not delete messages.

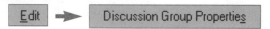

Notes:

- Use this procedure to manage disk space used by downloaded discussion group messages.

- You can set options to automatically delete both message text and headers after a specified length of time. Or, you can delete message text and keep message headers so that you can browse message headers. Then, at a later date, you can have Netscape Communicator delete old headers. For example, you could delete message text after 20 days and delete message headers after 30 days.

- Disk space options are set for each individual discussion group. That way, you can keep the messages for one group longer than those generated in another group.

Set Disk Space Options for Discussion Groups

1 Press **Ctrl+3** to open the Message Center window.

2 Click ⊞ next to the desired group server name to display the discussions groups on that server.

3 Right-click the discussion group to set properties.

4 Click **Discussion Group Properties** in the shortcut menu.

5 Click the **Disk Space** tab to display disk space options.

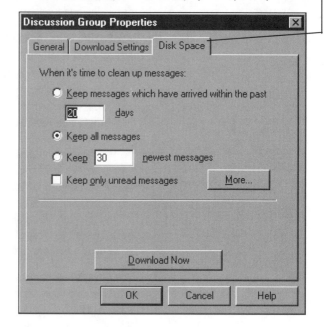

6 Select disk space options as desired:

- **Keep messages which arrived within the past x days.** Deletes messages based on the number of days since you last downloaded them.

- **Keep all messages**. Does not automatically delete messages.

- **Keep x newest messages**. Deletes messages based on how many new messages you have downloaded.

- **Keep only unread messages**. If you have set an option to delete messages, keeps all unread messages.

7 To set more disk space options if desired:

a. Click More to display the More Disk Space options dialog box.

b. Click **Remove message bodies** to delete the text of the message while leaving the message headers. That way you can browse headers offline without using the disk space required to store the entire message.

c. Type the number of **days** to store the entire message, including headers and message bodies. After the specified number of days, Netscape Communicator will delete message bodies.

d. Click OK.

8 Click OK.

Newsgroups: Send a Group Message

You can reply to group messages either privately by e-mail or by posting a message to the discussion group. You can also create new messages to post to the group or send privately.

File	➡	Open Discussion Group

Notes:

- Send private e-mail when your message wouldn't be of interest to group members. You can also post your reply to the group discussion.

- Netscape Communicator stores a copy of messages that you send to groups in the Sent folder, where e-mail messages that you send are also stored. To store group messages in a different folder, see **Newsgroups: Set Group Message Preferences**.

- You can send test messages to the *alt.test* group to make sure that your messaging is working properly.

Reply to a Group Message

1 Display the message.

> NOTE: *To display discussion group messages, go to the Message Center (Ctrl+3) and double-click the group name.*

2 Select a recipient:

- Press **Ctrl+R** to reply to the sender only (listed in the From: field of the original message) in the form of an e-mail message.

- Press **Ctrl+Shift+R** to send an e-mail message reply to the sender and any other recipients of the original message.

- Press **Ctrl+D** to post your reply to the discussion group.

- Press **Ctrl+Shift+D** to send an e-mail message to the sender and to post the message in the group discussion.

3 To change a recipient type if desired:

a. Click the recipient type box next to the name of the recipient to change in the message. A list of recipient types opens.

b. Click the new recipient type.

> NOTE: *For a description of recipient types, see E-Mail: Address an E-Mail Message. Followup-To recipients are used to cross-post a message to other groups that are following the message thread.*

196

4   Type your message.

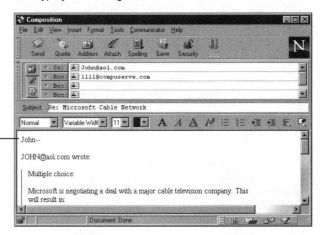

5   Click .

     NOTE: If you are working offline, the Send button shown above has a clock in the graphic displayed on the button. If you are working online, the Send button does not have the clock (see the illustration of the Composition window, above).

Create a New Group Message

1   Right-click the discussion group in the Message Center and click **New Message**.

2   Type your message.

3   Click .

Newsgroups: Set Download Options

Set up discussion groups to download whenever you go offline and specify which messages to download.

Edit ➝ Discussion Group Properties

Notes:

- Use this procedure to set discussion group download properties and to download discussion group messages.

- By default, discussion groups are not marked for downloading when you go offline. You select which discussion groups to download each time you go offline. However, using this procedure, you can mark a group to download by default. You can override the setting and then if you choose, download it when you go offline. See **Newsgroups: Work with Group Messages Offline** for more information.

- Discussion group properties also specify which messages to download. For example, you could download group messages from the last two days or the last two weeks. By default, Netscape Communicator downloads unread messages from the last week.

Set Download Properties for a Group/Download Messages

1   Open Message Center window (**Ctrl+Shift+1**).

2   Double-click the name of server to display discussion groups.

3   Right-click the discussion group to display group properties and select Discussion Group Properties.

4   Click the **Download Settings** tab.

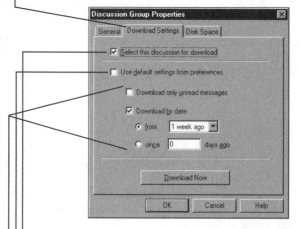

5   If you want to mark current group for downloading whenever you go offline, click **S̲elect this discussion for download** to select it.

  NOTE: When you go offline, you can choose not to download the group. See **Newsgroups: Work with Messages Offline**.

6   Specify which messages to download:
  - Select **Use d̲efault settings from preferences** to use default preferences settings. See **Set Default Download Options** in this section.
  OR
  - Use remaining options to specify which messages to download.

7 Click [OK] to save the settings.

OR

Click [Download Now] to save the settings and also download messages.

Set Default Download Options

1 Click **Edit**, **Preferences**.

2 Click the plus sign (⊞) next to **Offline** in the **Categories** list. Click **Download** to display download preferences.

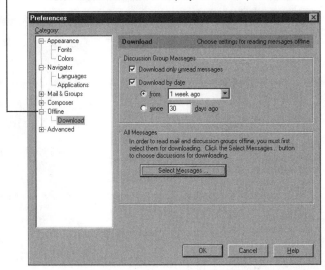

3 Set Discussion Group Messages options to specify which messages to download as desired.

4 To specify which discussion groups are marked for downloading whenever you go offline:

a. Click [Select Messages...].

b. Click the circle for each discussion group to download by default. A check mark is displayed next to groups marked for downloading.

c. Click [OK].

5 Click [OK] to close the Preferences dialog box.

199

Newsgroups: Set Group Message Preferences

You can automatically store a copy of all messages that you send to groups, store copies of messages in a particular folder, and include yourself as a recipient of messages that you send to groups.

Notes:

- This procedure only covers message preferences that apply to group messages (not e-mail messages). Group messages are messages that you post to a group discussion. See **E-mail: Set Outgoing Message Formatting Preferences.**

- You can specify whether or not to automatically send a copy to yourself (as a Bcc recipient) of all group messages that you send. A Bcc (blind carbon copy) recipient is not listed in the message header in the list of recipients. Recipients of your message will not see the Bcc recipient name. However, replies to the message are automatically sent to a Bcc recipient.

1 Click **Edit**, **Preferences**.

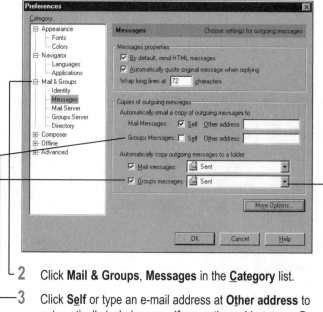

2 Click **Mail & Groups**, **Messages** in the **Category** list.

3 Click **Self** or type an e-mail address at **Other address** to automatically include yourself or another address as a Bcc recipient of all messages that you send to groups.

4 Click the **Groups messages** option to set whether or not Netscape Communicator automatically saves a copy of all messages that you send to groups.

5 Click the **Groups messages** drop-down arrow and select a different folder in which to store messages that you send to groups if desired.

NOTE: To create a new folder in the Message Center window to store messages, see **E-mail: Organize Messages in Folders.**

- In order to read newsgroup messages, you must first download them. To control how many messages are down-loaded automatically when you open a newsgroup, you can have Netscape Communicator display a prompt before downloading more than the maxi-mum number of messages that you specify. By default, Netscape Communicator prompts you before downloading more than 500 messages. You might, for exam-ple, want to down-load only 150 messages before you are prompted.

- By default, group messages that you send are stored in the Sent folder along with e-mail messages. You can specify a folder in which to store messages that you send to groups to keep them separate from e-mail.

─6 Click **Groups Server** in the **Category** list.

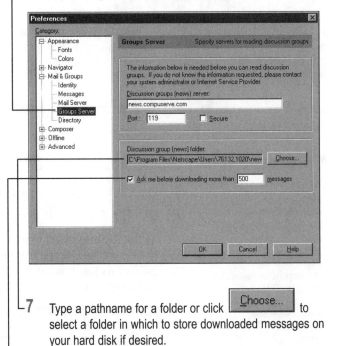

─7 Type a pathname for a folder or click Choose... to select a folder in which to store downloaded messages on your hard disk if desired.

─8 Select or deselect the **Ask me** option to have Netscape Communicator display a prompt before downloading more than the number of specified **messages**.

9 Click OK .

Newsgroups: Subscribe to a Discussion Group

To get involved in a newsgroup, you have to subscribe to it. After subscribing, you can download, read, and reply to messages. If a group no longer interests you, unsubscribe to remove yourself from the group. Newsgroups are called discussion groups in Netscape.

File ➡ Subscribe to Discussion Groups...

Notes:

- Before you can subscribe to a discussion group, you must have added the group server in Netscape Communicator. See **Newsgroups: Add a Group Server**. You can also add a server from the Subscribe to Discussion Groups dialog box. Click the **Add Server** button and enter the server location. Then, click the **Get Groups** button to display the groups on the server.

- Group servers and groups to which you are subscribed are listed in the Message Center.

- When you connect to a group server, Netscape Communicator searches for the groups on the server and displays them. While it is searching, the message, "Receiving discussion groups," appears in the status bar. When all groups are found and displayed, the message "Done" appears.

Subscribe to a Discussion Group

1 Press **Ctrl+3** to go to the Message Center.

2 Click **File**, **Subscribe to Discussion Groups**.

Netscape Communicator searches the group server (displayed in the **Server** box at the bottom of the dialog box) and displays the groups on the server. If it does not automatically search the server, click the **Get Groups** button.

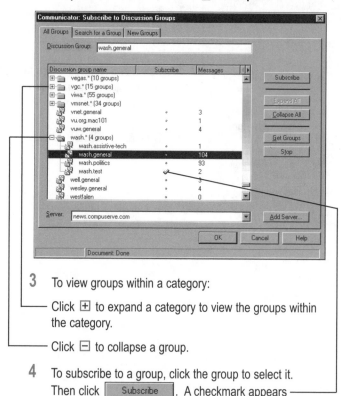

3 To view groups within a category:

Click ⊞ to expand a category to view the groups within the category.

Click ⊟ to collapse a group.

4 To subscribe to a group, click the group to select it. Then click [Subscribe]. A checkmark appears next to groups that you are subscribed to.

Notes:

- The list of news-groups on the server is probably quite long. To jump to a particular group in the list, type the group name in the **Discussion Group** text box at the top of the screen. To find discussion groups by searching for a particular topic, see **Newsgroups: Use DejaNews to Explore Usenet**. For an introduction to discussion groups, see **Newsgroups: An Overview**.

- You can check for new groups that have been added to a group server. Click the **New Groups** tab in the Subscribe to Discussion Groups dialog box (shown on the previous page). When you click **Get New** in the **New Groups** tab, Netscape Communicator finds all new groups that have been added to the server since you last clicked the **Clear New** button.

5   Click [OK   ].

6   To read and respond to group discussion messages, see **Newsgroups: Work with Group Messages**.

Unsubscribe

You can remove yourself from a discussion group from either the Subscribe to Discussion Groups dialog box shown in this section or from the Message Center, which lists groups to which you are subscribed.

- In the Subscribe to Discussion Groups dialog box (**File**, **Subscribe to Discussion Groups**), click the group and then click [Unsubscribe].
  OR
- In the Message Center (**Ctrl+3**), right-click the discussion group and click **Remove Discussion Group**.

Newsgroups: Work with Group Messages

Browse and read messages, get information about the author of a message, save the message in a file, print a message, and otherwise work with group messages.

File ➡ Open Discussion Group

Notes:

- Use the Netscape Discussion window to browse discussion group messages. Scroll through the list of message headers in the top pane of the window. When you see a message that interests you, click the message header to display the body of the message text in the bottom pane.

- From the Netscape Discussion window you can read messages, send replies, get information about the author, add the author to your address book, forward messages, and other functions.

Work with Messages in the Netscape Discussion Window

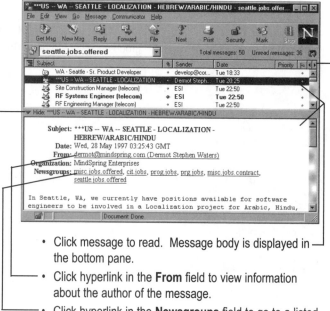

- Click message to read. Message body is displayed in the bottom pane.

- Click hyperlink in the **From** field to view information about the author of the message.

- Click hyperlink in the **Newsgroups** field to go to a listed newsgroup.

- Click the Hide arrow to close the bottom pane. Click again to reopen the pane (arrow appears in the status bar when the bottom pane is closed).

- Click to show more message header fields or click to hide fields.

- Click and select a folder to store a copy of the message in another folder. For more information, see **E-Mail: Organize Messages in Folders**.

204

More Ways to Work with Messages

Save, print, and copy messages in the Netscape Discussion window. You can also add the sender of a message to your address book.

- Click **Message**, **Add to Address Book**, **Sender** to add the sender of the message to your address book.
- Right-click a message header and click **Save Message** to save the message in a plain text file.
- Right-click a message header and click **Print Message** to print.
- Click **Message**, **Copy Message** and select a folder to save a copy of the message in another folder.

Newsgroups: Work with Group Messages Offline

After you subscribe to a group, you can read and send messages within the group. Use this procedure if you want to download messages from your group and go offline to read and respond to them. You can then, go back online to send your replies. To work with group messages online, see **Newsgroups: Work with Group Messages Online**.

Download Messages and Work Offline

1 Click **File**, **Go Offline** in the Message Center window. The Download dialog box appears.

2 Deselect the **Download Mail** and/or **Send Messages** options if you do not want to retrieve and send messages before you go offline.

NOTE: Leave the Download Discussion Groups option marked. This option must be selected if you wish to download discussion group messages to read offline.

- When you read messages offline, Netscape Communicator downloads both message headers and message text (when you work online it downloads only message headers). Since this can require a lot of disk space, you can set options for each discussion group that determine how often Netscape Communicator automatically deletes old messages in the group. See **Newsgroups: Remove Old Messages**.

- By default, Netscape Communicator does not download from newsgroups when you go offline. Using this procedure, you can specify which groups to download each time you go offline. To set up groups to download by default as well as how many messages to download (for example, all messages in the past two days), see **Newsgroups: Set Download Options**.

- You do not have to go offline to download messages. You can download messages at any time as described in **Newsgroups: Set Download Options**.

3 To select discussion groups to download:

a. Click [Select Items For Download...] to open the Discussion Groups dialog box.

NOTE: Discussion groups selected for downloading are checked in the Discussion Groups dialog box. By default, no discussion groups are marked.

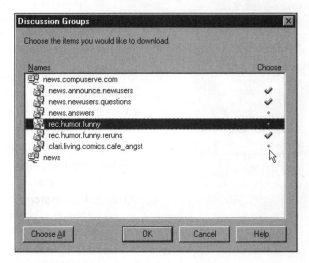

b. Click the circle to the right of each group to download. The circle changes to a checkmark.

c. Click [OK].

4 Click [Go Offline]. Netscape Communicator downloads messages and goes offline. Your network connection is still active.

   *NOTE: If the group has more than the number of messages specified in Preferences, the Download Headers dialog box displays. Specify the number of messages to download. You can only read messages that you download. To set the number of messages to automatically download, see **Newsgroups: Set Group Message Preferences**.*

5 To read and work with messages listed in the Message Center window:

   a. Click the ⊞ next to the server name to display discussion groups that you belong to.

   b. Double-click the discussion group to open.

   c. Browse, read, and reply to messages in the Netscape Discussion window.

   *NOTE: See **Newsgroups: Work with Group Messages** for tips on using the Message Center window to browse reply to and otherwise work with messages. Also see the E-mail sections of this book (procedures for group messages are very similar to those for e-mail messages. For example, to search through messages, see **E-mail Search Messages**.*

6 To go back online when finished working with messages:

   a. Click **File**, **Go Online**. The Download dialog box appears as described in step 2.

   b. Deselect options for any tasks that you do not want to perform in the Download dialog box.

   c. Click [Go Online].

Continue

Newsgroups: Work with Group Messages Online

After you subscribe to a group, you can read and send messages within the group. Use this procedure if want to stay online while you read and respond to messages. To work with group messages offline, see **Newsgroups: Work with Group Messages Offline**.

File ➡ Open Discussion Group

Notes:

- Use this procedure to open the messages in a discussion group of which you are a member. To be a member of a group, you must be subscribed to it as described in **Newsgroups: Subscribe to a Discussion Group**.

- The discussion group servers and the groups on each server that you are a member of are listed in the Message Center window. You access group messages from this window.

- When you read group messages online, Netscape Communicator downloads the header of each message. A message header contains information such as the subject and author of the message. You can then browse messages, copy them, reply to them, and otherwise work with group messages

Download Message Headers and Work Online

1   Press **Ctrl+Shift+1** to open the Message Center window.

2   Click ⊞ next to the discussion group server name to display a list of subscribed groups on the server.

3   Double-click the group to open.

4   If a group has more than 500 messages, Netscape Communicator displays the Download Headers dialog box where you can choose how many headers to download.

> *NOTE: By default, the Download Headers dialog box is displayed when there are more than 500 messages. You can change the number of messages that trigger this dialog box. For example, you might prefer to display the Download Headers dialog box if there are 250 messages. See **Newsgroups: Set Group Message Preferences**.*

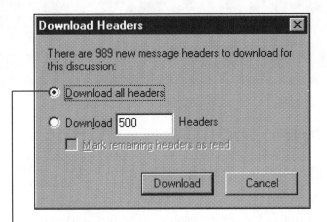

- If you will spend a lengthy amount of time working with messages, you can save money if your service provider does not charge you for time spent working offline. See **Newsgroups: Open Messages Offline** for more information.

- When you download, you are prompted for the number of messages to download in a group if the number of messages exceeds that set in Preferences. For example, if Preferences is set to automatically download 200 messages, you are not prompted if the group has only 150 messages. To set the number of messages to automatically download, see **Newsgroups: Set Group Message Preferences**.

- After you download message headers, you can read, respond to, file, search and otherwise work with messages. For information on working in the Message Center window, see **Newsgroups: Work with Group Messages**. Group messages are similar to e-mail messages. See also the E-mail sections of this book. For example, to search through messages, see **E-mail: Search Messages**.

Click **Download all headers** if you want to be able to read all messages, or type the number of headers that you want to download in the **Download Headers** text box. Then click the **Download** button.

NOTE: You can only read those messages whose headers you download.

5 To read messages in the Message Center window:

a. Click the ⊞ next to the server name to display discussions groups that you belong to.

b. Double-click the discussion group to open.

c. Double-click the message to open.

d. Browse, read, and reply to messages in the Netscape Discussion window.

211

Index

N

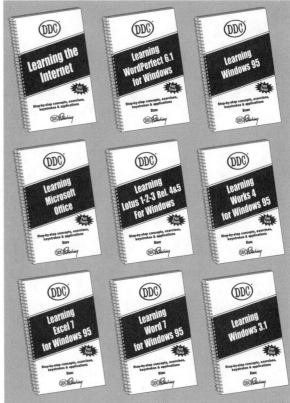